KW-053-777

Public Order:
A guide to the 1986 Public Order Act

Fourmat Publishing

Public Order:
A guide to the 1986 Public Order Act

by
John Marston LL.B, Solicitor,
Senior Lecturer in Law at Leicester Polytechnic

London
Fourmat Publishing
1987

ISBN 1 85190 024 1

First published January 1987

All rights reserved

© 1987 Fourmat Publishing
27 & 28 St Albans Place Islington Green London N1 ONX

Printed in England by Billing & Sons Limited, Worcester

Foreword

The 1986 Act is the most far-reaching and detailed legislative provision in the area of public order yet enacted. It does more than simply restate the 1936 Act. It represents the culmination of many years of debate and discussion both in and out of Parliament. As such the progress of the legislation was marked by lengthy debate on matters of principle and detail. But it is to be regretted that the opportunity was not taken to restate public order law more fully and to tidy up the miscellany of common law and other powers and offences which persist despite the passage of the Act, eg the breach of the peace preventive powers and duties of the police and the citizen. Consequently, the practitioner must look both to the detail of the Act and the common law and to a variety of matters in other statutes (including sections of the 1936 Act unaffected by the 1986 Act).

This text is intended to provide an explanatory guide to the 1986 Act and to some of the matters which will continue to provide a framework for the operation of the Act, eg the breach of the peace powers and obstruction of the highway. The Act is so wide-ranging as to impinge upon the lives and concerns of many individuals and groups - such as pressure groups, local authorities and landowners. Practitioners in all fields will be called upon to advise on the Act, whether it be in the Crown Courts, the magistrates' courts, local government or private practice. I hope they will find the text useful.

The Public Order Act 1986 (Commencement No 1) Order (SI 1986 No 2041) brings into force s.11 (advance notice of public processions), s.38 (tampering with goods) and Sch. 1 (amendments to the Sporting Events (Control of Alcohol etc) Act 1985) on 1 January 1987. The remaining substantive provisions of the Act are expected to become operative on 1 April 1987, although at the time of writing the commencement orders have not been made.

My thanks are due to Greg Knight MP who kindly helped me keep abreast of developments in Parliament and to Richard Ward of the School of Law, Leicester Polytechnic whose fertile imagination continues to assist me. Above all my gratitude is owed to Virginia who provided tea and comfortable advice and whose practical help and encouragement ensured the production of a typescript. All errors or omissions are the responsibility of both myself and Rusty without whose constant feline attentions I would the sooner have finished the text.

Leicester
December 1986

Contents

Table of Cases

Chapter 1

Introduction

1.1 Background to the legislation

The Public Order Act 1986 (referred to throughout this book as "the Act"):

- repeals much of the Public Order Act 1936 ("the 1936 Act");
- abolishes several common law offences;
- introduces new statutory offences to replace some of those common law offences abolished or statutory offences repealed;
- amends or repeals certain other statutory provisions, eg as to licensing and racial hatred;
- introduces several new powers in relation to offences committed at or in connection with football matches; and
- introduces miscellaneous provisions in relation to mass trespass and tampering with goods on sale.

The background to the Act is to be found in several wide-ranging documents. The Green Paper *Review of the Public Order Act 1936 and Related Legislation* (1980) (Cmnd 7891) initiated the move towards change but was, of course, only a preliminary discussion document. The Fifth Report of the House of Commons Homes Affairs Committee (*The Law Relating to Public Order* (1979-1980 HC 756)) was an influential report which dealt with many aspects of public order law and practice. It concentrated largely upon the statutory provisions relating to processions and assemblies. The Law Commission concentrated mainly upon the common

15

law offences, although some important and illuminating comments upon s.5 of the 1936 Act were made (see generally the Law Commission Report No 123 (*Offences Relating to Public Order*) and its Working Paper No 82). The Law Commission remarked that their report "..... does not purport to be a comprehensive review of all aspects of the law relating to public order".

The Government in its White Paper *The Review of Public Order Law* (Cmnd 9510) drew the strands together and made proposals which have been largely incorporated into the Act. Where appropriate reference is made in the text to these important sources. The courts are permitted to have recourse to some of these documents, at least for the purpose of identifying the mischief which was the concern of the legislators. The scope of the enquiry may be limited; for the permitted extent of judicial enquiry see *Assam Railways & Trading Ltd* v *IRC* and *Black Clawson* v *Papierwerke AG*. The latter case was marked by inconsistencies of approach. In *R* v *Allen* the House of Lords confirmed the accepted practice and said that the report and draft Bill of the Criminal Law Revision Committee might properly be considered by a court attempting to establish the mischief aimed at by the Act. More recently, in *R* v *Shivpuri*, Lord Bridge regretted that in an earlier case the House of Lords had not taken due note of what had been said in a Law Commission report; had they done so they would not have fallen into error. In the same case Lord Hailsham regretted the departure of the Act from the draft Bill produced by the Law Commission. Useful indications of purpose and explanation may be derived from these sources, especially the Law Commission Report.

1.2 The scheme of the Act in general

Part I introduces several new offences and abolishes or repeals several common law and statutory offences. Part II introduces new provisions for the control of processions and assemblies. Part III deals with racial hatred. Part IV deals with orders excluding individuals from football grounds. Part V deals with offences connected with the tampering with goods and mass trespass; in conjunction with Sch. 3 it makes changes to certain licensing provisions, and in conjunction with Sch. 2 it provides for amendments or repeals.

1.3 Geographical extent of the Act

Section 42 specifies precisely the extent of the Act. Generally, it applies only to England and Wales (s.42(1)) but s.42(2) extends parts of the Act to Scotland and s.42(3) extends part of the Act to Northern Ireland. The treatment within this text is intended to relate to matters affecting England and Wales only.

1.4 Repeals and abolitions

(a) The common law

The ancient common law offences of riot, rout, unlawful assembly and affray have been abolished (s.9(1)). Three offences have been created as replacements: riot (s.1); violent disorder (s.2) and affray (s.3). The Act does not affect other common law offences such as public nuisance, which may arise from time to time in public order cases.

(b) The 1936 Act

Amendments to the 1936 Act have been effected by s.40(3) (and see Sch. 3) and s.9(2)(d). Section 5 of the 1936 Act has been repealed, as has s.5A (inserted into that Act by s.70 Race Relations Act 1970). These sections dealt mainly with threatening, abusive or insulting words or behaviour either intended or likely to occasion a breach of the peace (s.5) or likely to stir up racial hatred (s.5A). In respect of s.5 two new offences have been created; see ss.4 and 5. Section 5A has been restructured and amended to produce six new offences; see ss.17 - 29. There have been consequential repeals of the provisions in the Theatres Act 1968 and Cable and Broadcasting Act 1984 dealing with racial hatred (and see Sch. 2 para. 5 for other minor consequential amendments to the Cable and Broadcasting Act 1984).

Section 4 of the 1936 Act (control of offensive weapons) has been repealed. The effect of this repeal will be negligible since the offence closely corresponded to s.1 Prevention of Crime Act 1959, in respect of which the maximum penalty is far greater. Section 3 of the 1936 Act (imposition of prohibition orders and conditions on processions) has been repealed and replaced by a new provision of greater scope and effect, including an advance notice provision and the extension of the condition-making power to certain public assemblies. Offences in connection with advance notice, breach of conditions or prohibition orders are, of course, included in the Act (ss.11 - 14). The offences of wearing in a public place a uniform signifying association with any political organisation or the promotion of any political objective (s.1), and organising, training etc quasi military organisations (s.2), are unaffected by the Act. See *O'Moran* v *DPP*, where the meaning of "uniform" was considered. A power of arrest for offences under ss.1 and 2 was preserved by the Police and Criminal Evidence Act 1984 Sch. 2. See also Prevention of Terrorism (Temporary Provisions) Act 1984, ss.1, 2, 7 and 10 which deal with similar matters.

(c) Other statutory offences

The Act repeals in their entirety several unimportant Acts which created offences and which had fallen into desuetude (s.9(2) and Sch. 3): Tumultuous Petitioning Act 1661; Shipping Offences Act 1793; Seditious Meetings Act 1817.

Two offences identified by the Law Commission as probably having fallen into disuse have been repealed in part:

- the part of s.4 Vagrancy Act 1824 dealing with possession of offensive weapons has been repealed; see Sch. 3. Whilst s.4 of the 1824 Act was held to apply to conduct in private places, s.3 Prevention of Crime Act 1953 applies only to public places;
- s.54 (para. 13) Metropolitan Police Act 1839 and s.35 City of London Police Act 1839 have been repealed. These created summary offences of threatening, abusive or insulting behaviour which were the

forerunners of s.5 of the 1936 Act; the maximum punishment was a very small fine. Section 54 was often used in cases where s.5 of the 1936 Act was thought to be inappropriate, eg because of the small maximum penalty available (for an example of its use see *Masterson* v *Holden*).

There is, of course, in Sch. 3 a wide range of other amendments or repeals including the repeal of a number of local Acts dealing with provisions as to notice of processions.

1.5 Specific amendments effected by Schedule 2

Section 7 Conspiracy and Protection of Property Act 1875: for details and discussion of the offence of intimidation see page 127. By Sch. 2 para. 1(2) there is added to s.7 a power for a constable to arrest anyone he reasonably suspects is committing the offence. Schedule 2 para. 1(1) increases the penalty for the offence.

Section 1 Prevention of Crime Act 1953 (possession of offensive weapons in a public place): s.1(4) is amended by Sch. 2 para. 2 of the Act to bring it into line with the definition of prohibited article in s.1(9) Police and Criminal Evidence Act 1984. The definition of offensive weapon now reads (with the amendment in italics):

"..... any article made or adapted for use for causing injury to the person, or intended by the person having it with him for such use by him *or by some other person.*"

The amendment to s.1(4) means that where A is in possession of an item for use not by himself but by B, then A will be guilty of the offence as principal.

Save for this minor change the offence is unaffected by the Act.

The Criminal Justice Act 1982 is amended by the addition of the offences under ss.1-3 to Sch. 1 Part II of the 1982 Act (offences excluded from the provisions in that Act as to early release).

There are minor amendments to the *Cable and Broadcasting Act 1984* (see Sch. 2 para. 5).

The Police and Criminal Evidence Act 1984 s.17(1)(c) is amended by Sch. 2 para. 7; there is a new power to enter in order to arrest a person reasonably suspected of an offence under s.4 of the Act. There was previously in s.17(1)(c) a power to enter premises in connection with s.5 of the 1936 Act.

1.6   Other offences

It must always be remembered that the powers in the Act will be operated against the background of far wider powers under the more general criminal law and that a wide range of offences may be committed in situations of public disorder. Discussion of this range of offences is beyond the scope of this book and reference should be made to the standard texts for discussion of such offences as assault, criminal damage, public nuisance, offences under the Explosive Substances Act 1893 and assault or wilful obstruction of a constable in the execution of his duty. There is, in addition, a wide range of public order offences independent of the Act. Some of these, including some less well known, will be discussed at various points in the text.

1.7   The new offences

The following offences will be dealt with in Chapter 3:

- entry to premises in breach of an exclusion order (s.32(3));
- offences in connection with alcohol, with licensing and with fireworks etc (Sch. 1);
- tampering with articles on sale;
- the offence in connection with mass trespass.

The following offences will be dealt with in Chapter 4:

- riot (s.1);
- affray (s.2);
- violent disorder (s.3).

The following offences will be dealt with in Chapter 5:

- threatening, abusive or insulting words or behaviour (or display or distribution of writing) intended or likely to provoke violence or cause fear of violence (s.4);
- threatening, abusive or insulting words, behaviour or display of writing or disorderly behaviour likely to cause harassment, alarm or distress (s.5); this conduct as a whole can best be described as "offensive conduct".
- offences in connection with incitement to racial hatred (ss.18 - 23).

The following offences will be dealt with in Chapter 6:

- organiser of procession failing to give notice or to adhere to the details in the notice (s.11(7));
- failure to comply with condition imposed on a procession (s.12 (4), (5), (6));
- participating in or organising a prohibited procession (s.13(7), (8), (9));
- organising or participating in an assembly in breach of conditions imposed (s.14(4), (5), (6)).

Insofar as the new offences introduced by the Act are concerned, it is likely that the practitioner will soon become familiar with the successors to s.5 of the 1936 Act (see ss.4 and 5, Chapter 5) and these offences will undoubtedly be charged on frequent occasions in much the same way as s.5 of the 1936 Act. "Riot" is likely to be something of a rarity but "violent disorder" and "affray" may be relatively common offences, especially the former which no longer requires proof of any common purpose. Riot still requires proof of a common purpose. Opportunity has also been taken in the Act to increase the powers of the courts and police in respect of offences in connection with football matches and "mass trespass". The Sporting Events (Control of Alcohol etc) Act 1985 has been amended extensively by the addition of new offences (see Sch. 1 and Chapter 3) and new licensing provisions (see Sch. 1). In addition, there is now a power in the courts to make an order that a person convicted of certain offences should be excluded from football grounds and that he (or she) should have his photograph taken (see ss.30 -37 and Chapter 3). There are also new powers for the police in certain circumstances to issue a direction that trespassers leave property, and there is an offence in connection with this power (see s.39 and Chapter 3).

Some of the provisions of the Act are procedural in nature (although subject to criminal sanction for breach) and from time to time the practitioner will be called upon to advise on matters in relation to which these provisions will be in issue, eg the advance notice requirement in s.11, and the new licensing provisions. Local practice upon these matters may vary.

1.8 Local Acts and bye-laws

Historically many local Acts contained provisions either requiring the consent of the local authority to certain processions (eg s.94 Leicester Act 1956) or advance notice of processions. Several such Acts survived despite the 1972 Local Government Act and laid down advance notice provisions; see for example, County of South Glamorgan Act 1976 s.25; County of Merseyside Act 1980 s.31; West Midlands County Council Act 1980 s.38; Cheshire County Council Act 1980 s.28; Isle of Wight Act 1980 s.26; Greater Manchester Act 1980 s.56; East Sussex Act 1981 s.29. These provisions have largely been repealed by Sch. 3. However, certain sections have not been repealed. These sections create a requirement for the drawing by the police of a code of practice. The sections are in almost identical terms and create a code of practice requirement in the counties of Greater Manchester, Cheshire, Isle of Wight and West Midlands.

In the appendices will be found the Act, a specimen "banning order" made under the 1936 Act and the code of practice made by the West Midlands police under local Act of Parliament. It would appear to be appropriate, although not obligatory, for other police forces, which did not have a local requirement for advance notice of processions, to seek similar information in addition to that to which they are entitled under the terms of the Act.

In addition, there are likely to be in many areas bye-laws which may be applicable to the conduct of processions or otherwise affect demonstrations, eg as to the display of posters, the use of loud-hailers, the distribution of handbills (for example in parts in Leicester it is an offence to "distribute any handbill, notice, book or other written or printed matter to the annoyance of any other person using the park"). Bye-laws commonly restrict the holding of meetings in certain places or require consent to meetings and assemblies. Bye-laws and local Acts often contain provisions which make disorderly or offensive behaviour or conduct which causes annoyance an offence (see *Nash* v *Finlay*).

1.9 Breach of the peace

The Act is not a comprehensive code on the law relating to public order. Whilst certain common law offences have been abolished and certain statutory provisions have been repealed or amended, much of the pre-Act law remains intact. In this respect it is important to note that the common law powers to deal with or prevent breaches of the peace are unaffected by the Act (s.40(4)). This is in line with the approach taken in ss.17, 24 and 26, Police and Criminal Evidence Act 1984 - powers to arrest for breaches of the peace are unaffected and powers to enter premises to deal with breaches of the peace are expressly preserved. Consequently, it is opportune and necessary to review in Chapter 2 the common law powers to prevent or deal with breaches of the peace.

1.10 Binding over

The powers of the court and magistrates to bind over to keep the peace or be of good behaviour under the Justice of the Peace Act 1361 or the Magistrates' Courts Act 1980 are unaffected by the Act.

Chapter 2

Common law preventive powers and duties

2.1 Introduction

As has already been seen, the Act does not establish a comprehensive code of powers to control or prevent public disorder. Reference must continue to be made to common law powers to deal with or prevent breaches of the peace. It is often the case that the common law preventive powers arise in the context of an offence under s.51 Police Act 1964 (assault or wilful obstruction of a constable acting in the execution of his duty), or in an action for damages for trespass to the person. Whether a police officer is acting in the execution of his duty will often be answered by asking whether or not he is acting to control a breach of the peace; that this elementary point is often overlooked can be seen in the House of Lords decision in *Albert* v *Lavin*.

2.2. Common law preventive powers and duties

Section 40(4) is quite clear: "Nothing in this Act affects the common law powers in England and Wales to deal with or prevent a breach of the peace." The full range of preventive powers based upon actual or apprehended breaches of the peace is preserved. The Police and Criminal Evidence Act 1984 adopted a similar approach to powers of arrest and entry. It is important to note that despite the development of wider powers of arrest in the Police and Criminal Evidence Act 1984 the arrest powers for breach of the peace and the preventive powers in connection with actual or apprehended breaches of the peace will continue to play an important role in the exercise of police powers. It is too early to condemn these powers to the backwaters of academic consideration. The powers will continue to be especially relevant to supplement the provisions in ss.11-16 for the control of processions and assemblies.

2.3 Duties in connection with a breach of the peace

The common law imposes a duty on all citizens to suppress breaches of the peace. This duty is of ancient origin and is illustrated by clear and uncompromising statements in the *Bristol Riots Case*, *R* v *Pinney* and *R* v *Kennett*. The authoritative statement of the House of Lords in *Albert* v *Lavin* (see page 32) indicates both the nature of the obligation upon the citizen and the steps which may be taken to deal with breaches of the peace which are occurring or are about to occur in his presence. It is an offence for a citizen to fail to come to the assistance of a constable when that constable apprehends a breach of the peace and there is reasonable necessity for calling on the citizen to assist (see *R* v *Brown*). There is a defence of physical impossibility or lawful excuse although the scope of the defence is uncertain. The Royal Commission on Criminal Procedure (Cmnd 8092) indicated that there have been prosecutions for this offence even in modern times. The importance of the duty is that it is placed upon every citizen and that in acting to suppress breaches of the peace police officers and others will be acting lawfully.

2.4 What is a breach of the peace?

The Act has preferred to base many of the new offences on the concept of "unlawful violence", and does not rely on "breach of the peace". However, the common law continues to depend upon this ill-defined but useful concept; it was referred to by the draftsman of the Draft Criminal Code as "a somewhat vague notion". In England and Wales breach of the peace is not a substantive offence, unlike Scotland which recognises it as a crime. The courts have consistently refused to provide a definition of breach of the peace although the Court of Appeal in *R* v *Howell* considered that:

" ..... there is a breach of the peace whenever harm is actually done or is likely to be done to a person or in his presence to his property or a person is in fear of being so harmed through an assault, an affray, a riot, unlawful assembly or other disturbance."

A disturbance not involving violence or the fear of violence will not be a breach of the peace. The statement in *R* v *Howell* was approved, by the Court of Appeal, in *Parkin* v *Norman* and was preferred to the following *dictum* of Lord Denning in *R* v *Chief Constable for Devon and Cornwall ex parte Central Electricity Generating Board*, whose observations are too wide for general application:

"I think that the conduct of these people ..... is itself a breach of the peace. There is a breach of the peace whenever a person who is lawfully carrying out his work is unlawfully and physically prevented by another from doing it ...... if anyone unlawfully and physically obstructs the worker, by lying down or chaining himself to a rig or the like, he is guilty of a breach of the peace."

There is a close correlation between "violence" (as defined in s.8) and breach of the peace, although the latter may be more flexible in its application. For example the type of disturbance in the older cases such as *Howell* v *Jackson*, *Ingle* v *Bell*, *Cohen* v *Huskisson*, *Webster* v *Watts* (where the breach of the peace was seen to arise from the gathering of a crowd which because of its size and general manner threatened the peace) would not readily fall within ss.1 - 4 in the absence of actual threats or use of violence. Certainly great care is needed when reliance is placed on the older cases and in *R* v *Howell* Watkins LJ observed that "the older cases are of considerable interest but they are not a sure guide to what the term is understood to mean today .....".

2.5 Can lawful action amount to an actual breach of the peace?

This question should not be confused with the other important issue of whether or not a constable may restrict or terminate a lawful activity when he reasonably apprehends an imminent breach of the peace. Lord Denning in the *CEGB* case seemed to suggest that lawfulness is irrelevant to the issue of whether or not a breach of the peace exists: "But in deciding whether there is a breach of the peace ..... the law does not go into the rights and wrongs of the matter, or whether it is justified by self help or not." Despite this *dictum*, which was unsupported by the other members of the Court of Appeal, it is suggested that in the absence of unlawful violence (or threat thereof) no breach of the peace can be said to occur. In normal circumstances any exchange of violence will inevitably involve a breach of the peace, even if one of the parties is acting lawfully. In deciding whether or not there is a breach of the peace the courts are not concerned with allocating responsibility, there need only be some unlawful activity involving violence or threat thereof. Responsibility is an issue which needs to be considered only at the stage of deciding what action is reasonable and appropriate.

In *Marsh* v *Arscott*, a struggle occurred when an individual attempted to eject police officers from his property. McCullough J remarked:

> "..... the police officers, having been told to leave, were acting unlawfully in remaining. If the defendant was using no more force than was reasonably necessary to evict them he was acting lawfully, and in arresting him the police were acting unlawfully. This violent incident amounted to a breach of the peace but it was one for which the police officers were responsible and not the defendant himself ..... Suppose ..... that the defendant's threats and use of force towards the police had been unlawful, once again there would have been a breach of the peace. In this event the defendant would have been responsible for breaching the peace. Thus, regardless of

who was acting lawfully and who was acting unlawfully there was at the time of the incident a breach of the peace."

This approach can also be seen in *Joyce* v *Hertfordshire Constabulary*. The court decided that one police officer could intervene in a struggle between the appellant and another police officer and need not be certain that there had been a lawful arrest. The court observed that "What was going on was in fact a struggle and a breach of the peace and the rights and wrongs do not matter." In *McBean* v *Parker* Dunn LJ said, of the requirement in *R* v *Howell* of the need for "harm", that it seemed to him that " ..... the harm done or likely to be done must be unlawful harm".

The problem with Lord Denning's approach is that it is difficult to see why a perfectly lawful action should be classified as a breach of the peace and therefore be liable to intervention. Can the removal of a trespasser under the common law power of self help be a breach of the peace where the trespasser does not struggle? Professor Leigh, in *Police Powers in England & Wales,* remarks that "it is, surely, absurd to postulate a breach of the peace on the part of the person using lawful force and then to use this as a pretext for exercising powers against those, however peaceful they may be against whom force is being used." Of course, this is not to say that the actions of removing demonstrators may not, in appropriate circumstances, give rise to a reasonable anticipation that a breach of the peace will occur. Whether it does or not was discussed somewhat inconclusively by the Court of Appeal in the *CEGB* case.

2.6 Reasonably apprehended breaches of the peace

Action may be taken not only in relation to breaches of the peace which are actually occurring but also in respect of reasonably apprehended imminent breaches of the peace. The difficulties of identifying the risk of breaches of the peace can be seen from the disparate views of the court in the *CEGB* case. Lord Denning accepted the possibility that the simple obstruction of the Board's employees might give rise to a reasonable apprehension of a breach of the peace. But Lawton LJ did not see any risk of a breach of the peace in mere removal of the protestors:

"..... police officers ..... cannot act unless they see a breach of the peace or have reasonable cause for suspecting that there is a real and imminent risk of one occurring ..... If those obstructing do allow themselves to be removed without struggling or causing an uproar (which seems to me unlikely .....) the police will have no reason for taking action, nor should they."

On the other hand, Templeman LJ took the view that:

"An obstructor who will not leave the site unless he is forcibly removed presents a threat and danger of a breach of the peace even if he disclaims any intention of causing a breach of the peace".

In any event, he went on to say:

".... the police will be entitled to intervene if an obstructor resists being carried away from the site or runs to another part of the site or tries to return to the site, thus obliging the board's representatives to seize him so that he may be permanently excluded. Such conduct by an obstructor ..... will create an imminent and serious danger of a breach of the peace for which the obstructor will be responsible and liable to arrest or removal by the police."

Whether a breach of the peace is reasonably apprehended as imminent is a question of fact and the courts have been reluctant to interfere with this decision. The belief as to the imminence of the breach of the peace must not only be honest but also be founded on reasonable grounds. *Piddington* v *Bates*, *Kavanagh* v *Hiscock* and *Tynan* v *Balmer* demonstrate the application of the common law principle and the general reluctance of courts to "second guess" police officers in these matters. Lord Parker in *Piddington* v *Bates* emphasizes both the need for grounds for the constable's reasonable belief and a real, not a remote, possibility of a breach of the peace. Lawton and Templeman LJJ both refer in the *CEGB* case to the need for a "real and imminent risk" or "imminent and serious danger" of a breach of the peace (see also *Moss* v *McLachan*, page 34: "The possibility of a breach must be real to justify any preventive action. The imminence or immediacy of the threat to the peace determines what action is reasonable.").

2.7 What steps may be taken in pursuance of the preventive duty?

The steps in *(a)* and *(b)* below are open to both ordinary citizens and the police, and reasonable force may be used. A constable who is acting within this preventive capacity is within the execution of his duty for the purposes of s.51(1) and (3) Police Act 1964 (assaulting and wilfully obstructing a constable in the execution of his duty). Even where the constable is doing something which at law he is not compelled to do he may still be acting in the execution of his duty, all the more so if he anticipates a breach of the peace: see *Coffin* v *Smith* (attending a youth club whose leader is ejecting youths). Equally, steps taken in performance of the preventive duty will constitute a defence to any civil action which may be brought against the constable or the chief constable.

(a) Arrest

The leading authority in this area is *R* v *Howell* where Watkins J drew together many of the older authorities and remarked:

"..... there is a power of arrest for breach of the peace where (1) a breach of the peace is committed in the presence of the person making the arrest, or (2) the arrestor reasonably believes that such a breach will be committed in the immediate future by the person arrested although he has not yet committed any breach, or (3) where a breach has been committed and it is reasonably believed that a renewal of it has been threatened."

31

There may also be a power to arrest in fresh pursuit of someone who has committed a breach of the peace; see *R v Light*, *R v Walker*.

Arrest would be with a view to taking a person before a magistrate to be bound over, or perhaps as a preliminary to a charge on a substantive offence, eg assault. A statement that the arrest is for a breach of the peace will be sufficient for all these eventualities and satisfy the requirements of s.28 Police and Criminal Evidence Act 1984.

(b) Other steps

The general proposition is that the citizen may take reasonable steps to deal with or prevent actual or reasonably apprehended imminent breaches of the peace; see *Albert v Lavin*:

" ..... every citizen in whose presence a breach of the peace is being, or reasonably appears to be about to be, committed has the right to take reasonable steps to make the person who is breaking or threatening to break the peace refrain from so doing."

Accordingly, police officers have been held to be entitled to act in a wide variety of ways which would normally involve serious interference with the liberty of the individual. The same powers may apply where a breach of the peace is likely to be renewed; see *Price v Seeley*, *Baynes v Brewster*, *Timothy v Simpson*; or where there is fresh pursuit; see *R v Marsden*.

It is possible to restrain someone and detain him for as long as reasonable to prevent the breach of the peace or its recurrence; see *Albert v Lavin*.

In connection with premises, there is power to enter premises to deal with actual breaches of the peace (see *Robson v Hallett*). Ejection from premises is another example. Even in those cases where a breach of the peace is not actually occurring but is apprehended as likely to occur, the power to enter and remain on premises exists: see *Thomas* v *Sawkins, McGowan* v *Chief Constable of Hull, R* v *Thornley*.

Many cases illustrate the wider proposition that police officers may do what is reasonable to prevent breaches of the peace which are occurring or which are reasonably apprehended as imminent. In *Duncan* v *Jones* the holding of a meeting on the highway (although not alleged to have been an obstruction of the highway) was reasonably apprehended as likely to lead to breaches of the peace. A refusal to comply with the request of the police officer to disperse amounted to a wilful obstruction of that constable (see also *O'Kelly* v *Harvey*). In *Duncan* v *Jones* it was said:

"..... the respondent reasonably apprehended a breach of the peace. It then ..... became his duty to prevent anything which in his view would cause that breach of the peace. While he was taking steps so to prevent a reasonably apprehended breach of the peace he was wilfully obstructed by the appellant."

The statements in certain of the earlier cases that the preventive action should be a matter of last resort or necessity appear not to have been relied upon in more recent authorities where the reasonableness of the action appears to be the major consideration in deciding the lawfulness of the action.

The use of preventive powers is frequently seen in the policing of pickets. The Code of Practice on picketing, issued under the Employment Act 1980, observes:

"26. ...... The law gives the police discretion to take whatever measures may reasonably be considered necessary to ensure that picketing remains peaceful and orderly.
28. It is for the police to decide, taking into account all the circumstances, whether the number of pickets at any particular place is likely to lead to a breach of the peace. If a picket does not leave the picket line when asked to do so by the police, he is liable to be arrested for obstruction

either of the highway or of a police officer in the execution of his duty if the obstruction is such as to cause, or be likely to cause, a breach of the peace."

Piddington v *Bates* (where the power was used to limit the number of pickets), *Kavanagh* v *Hiscock* (preventing pickets from approaching vehicles) and *Tynan* v *Balmer* demonstrate the application of the common law principles underlying the Code of Practice.

Most recently in the miners' strike of 1984 the discretion of the police extended to preventing pickets from journeying to the site of certain coal mines. At what precise stage such actions are unjustifiable will be a matter of fact. There may be some distinction between such directions being given 105 miles from a site and those given 5 miles from a site. In *Moss* v *McLachlan*, the road check was one and one half miles from two collieries and four miles from two other collieries. The roadchecks were lawful because of the reasonable apprehension of a breach of the peace. The police had reason to believe that striking miners stopped at road checks were on their way to picket *en masse* one or more of the collieries and that there would be a breach of the peace should they be allowed to continue. The miners refused to obey a direction to turn back and were arrested for obstructing the police in the execution of their duty. The appellants were held to have been properly convicted since the direction has been properly given by the police acting in the execution of their duty.

When appropriate the discretion of constables may extend to the removal of articles designed or likely to lead to breaches of the peace. In *Humphries* v *Connor*, the seizure of a provocative lily was held to be justified because of the reasonable anticipation of a breach of the peace. Placards, banners, flags, emblems and similar objects might be seized on this basis or directions given as to their use. Breach of these directions would amount to wilful obstruction of a constable in the execution of his duty contrary to s.51(3) Police Act 1964.

2.8   Against whom should the action be taken?

The courts appear to expect that the police will take action against the party "responsible" when that person can clearly be identified, eg in the *CEGB* case Lord Denning MR and the other members of the Court of Appeal clearly had it in mind that the police would operate only against the obstructors as the party "responsible". It should be noted that in the exercise of their preventive powers, the police are not restricted to action only against those "responsible"; they may also take action against anyone who is acting otherwise lawfully; see *Humphries v Connor*.

In *McBean v Parker* a police officer intervened to stop a struggle between the appellant and his colleague who was attempting to carry out an unlawful search of the appellant. The police officer was present throughout the stop and attempted search and could not be said to have been acting in the execution of his duty to prevent a breach of the peace since he knew that the initial detention had been unlawful. Dunn LJ said that:

"in a situation of this kind where two officers are involved and all that was needed was for the appellant to be told the reason for the search to make what was done lawful, it follows that if, thereafter, the person who is apprehended uses reasonable force to repel a search by one officer he is doing nothing unlawful. The other officer ..... cannot be said to be acting in the execution of his duty if he then attempts to restrain him ...... I will limit my decision to those facts."

But if a police officer comes across a struggle between an individual and another police officer he can intervene, since there is a breach of the peace. In *Joyce v Hertfordshire Constabulary*, at a football match, the police officer responsible for the initial detention of the defendant, with whom he then had a struggle, could not be identified. Another constable saw the struggle as part of a general and violent disturbance involving a group of fans and intervened to seize the defendant who struggled with him. The defendant was charged with conduct contrary to s.5 of the 1936 Act. The defence suggested that since the initial struggle was a result of an unlawful detention, the defendant had simply been using reasonable force to escape and the second officer should not have intervened.

The Divisional Court saw no merit in this view and made two points: (i) the court had been entitled to assume that the first detention was lawful; (ii) even if it had been unlawful, there was still a breach of the peace and the officer to whose attention it came was obliged to intervene: "What was going on was in fact a struggle and a breach of the peace and the rights and wrongs do not matter." In intervening the officer was acting in the execution of his duty and further struggles by the individual amounted to threatening behaviour and to offences contrary to s.51 Police Act 1964.

An individual who is in fact freeing himself from an unlawful detention may well find himself in difficulties vis-à-vis all but that constable and any other who may be tainted with the illegality of his colleague. A constable who comes across a general mêlée, in which it is possible that some of the parties will be acting in self-defence, need not assess who is responsible and may proceed against all concerned since there is a breach of the peace; see *Timothy* v *Simpson*:

> "If no-one could be restrained of his liberty in cases of mutual conflict, except the party who did the first wrong, and the bystanders acted at their peril in this respect, there would be very little chance of the public peace being preserved by the interference of private individuals ..... [or] of peace officers .....".

The possibility of abuse of the preventive power was noted in *Humphries* v *Connor*. Fitzgerald J was reluctant to agree with his colleagues because he thought that the police ought not to act against those who are carrying out lawful acts which others find displeasing and use as an excuse to break the peace. Rather, the police should act against those who threaten to, or who actually break the peace. To do otherwise would, in his view, make "the law of the mob supreme". O'Brien J perceived that there was a risk and specifically excluded abuse of power from the scope of his decision:

> "Our decision would not be applicable to a state of facts where the power was abused; and ...... it would not protect any constable from any unnecessary, excessive, or improper exercise of such power in other cases."

Chapter 3

Tampering with goods; trespass; football matches

3.1 Introduction

In this Chapter the following will be examined:

(i) offences in connection with tampering with goods;
(ii) the provisions on "mass trespass";
(iii) the extensive changes to the licensing provisions and offences contained in the Sporting Events (Control of Alcohol etc) Act 1985; and
(iv) the new provisions granting powers to magistrates in relation to offences at or in connection with football matches.

3.2 Contamination of or interference with goods (s.38)

The Criminal Damage Act 1971 remains unaffected by the Act, but s.38 contains provisions which might sit more happily in that Act rather than a Public Order Act. Section 38 creates new offences to deal with those who seek to promote a cause or objective by tampering with products supplied to the public or by claiming to have done so. Such tampering or claim must be accompanied by one of the intentions specified in s.38(1). There have been examples of campaigns against particular manufacturers or stores within this country but extreme examples of this sort of offence may be drawn from America and Japan, where deaths occurred. The problem in the United Kingdom is apparently on the increase and each police force has arrangements to co-ordinate measures in the event of occurrences of this nature.

(a) The offences

Both before and after the Act offences contrary to any of the following Acts may have been committed by those who tamper with goods:

    (i) blackmail contrary to the Theft Act 1968 s.21;

    (ii) administering a noxious substance contrary to the Offences Against the Person Act 1861 ss.23 and 24;

    (iii) criminal damage under the Criminal Damage Act 1971 s.1(1) & (2).

Where death or serious injury occurs then other offences may have been committed. All these offences present difficulties, eg as to *mens rea*. In criminal damage for instance, it will frequently be the case that the property damaged is that of the defendant and there may be difficulty in establishing the necessary *mens rea*. In any event the offences are not principally designed to combat the mischief against which the Act is designed to operate, ie the creation of apprehension amongst consumers or the general public by actual or claimed tampering.

It is now an offence for a person:

    (i)   to contaminate or interfere with goods (or to make it appear that goods have been contaminated or interfered with) (s.38(1)); or

    (ii) to place goods which have been (or which appear to have been) contaminated or interfered with in a place where such goods are supplied (s.38(1)); or

    (iii) to threaten that he, or another, will do either of (i) or (ii), or to claim that he or another has done so (s.38(2)).

The offences in (i) and (ii) require a specific intention to:

    (a) cause public alarm or anxiety (s.38(1)(a)); or

(b) cause injury to members of the public consuming or using the goods (s.38(1)(b)); or

(c) cause economic loss to any person by reason of the goods being shunned by members of the public (s.38(1)(c)); or

(d) cause economic loss to any person by reason of steps taken to avoid such alarm, anxiety, injury or loss (s.38(1)(d)).

The offence in (iii) above requires an intention under (a), (c) or (d).

It is also an offence to be in possession, with a view to the commission of an offence under s.38(1), of:

(a) materials to be used to contaminate or interfere with goods or to make it appear that goods have been contaminated or interfered with; or

(b) goods which have been or which appear to have been contaminated or interfered with.

The offences are triable on indictment with a maximum sentence on indictment of 10 years. They are therefore arrestable offences under s.24 Police and Criminal Evidence Act 1984. The offences are also triable summarily with a maximum term of imprisonment of six months and a fine or both (s.38(4)).

(b) Comment

"Contaminate"; "interfere"

These are left undefined and ought to receive a common-sense and broad interpretation. They are wider than damage and will cover instances ranging from (a) the addition of a harmless but discolouring substance; (b) the addition of an adhesive label to a package or item indicating that it may have been tampered with; (c) the injection of a harmful substance into food; (d) the removal or damage of part of a product so as to create a danger, eg in an electrical item.

"Goods"

This term is partially explained in s.38(5); that definition has been used in previous legislation (see for example the Consumer Safety Act 1978). Since it includes "substances natural or manufactured incorporated into goods or not, or mixed with goods or not", it is wide enough to encompass ingredients or parts for incorporation into another product. Thus goods during all stages of the manufacturing, processing, cleaning, production, storage, and sale stages are protected. The Act may well extend to growing crops.

The term "goods" may not be interpreted to include part of a building, so that, for example, interference with a lift will fall outside the Act, although the degree of annexation to the land may be relevant, eg may a fire extinguisher in a building be described as goods? A claim that a circus big top has been damaged, or that apparatus in a fair has been interfered with seems to fall within the mischief of causing public anxiety and economic loss. Whether such instances fall within the meaning of "goods" is unclear.

"place goods ..... where goods ..... are ..... otherwise supplied"

The "placing" offence seems to create a genus of places where goods are supplied. The supply need not be to the general public or to members of the public, but the necessary *mens rea* must be demonstrated. Where a person places contaminated goods on a production line, eg on a conveyor belt leading to a packing system, he should be charged, eg with "contamination" or "possession" rather than "placing", since the place will not be one where goods are "consumed, used, sold or otherwise supplied". The "placing" offence seems to be aimed at the deposit of goods on supermarket shelves, in cafes, in warehouses etc.

"the public"; "members of the public"

The mischief appears to be the creation of public alarm or anxiety, injury to members of the public, economic loss through public shunning of the goods or economic loss suffered in the avoidance of these matters. Where there is a campaign aimed at, say, a particular company and the intention is to cause alarm, anxiety, injury to that company's employees or economic loss through steps taken to prevent that alarm etc, then it may be difficult to hold that the employees of the company in question are "the public" or "members of the public" for this purpose.

(c) Good faith defence (s.38(6))

It has been thought necessary to include a good faith defence to the offence under s.38(2). Where a newspaper or TV or radio company reports a publicly acknowledged claim of interference or contamination it is hard to envisage a prosecution, let alone a successful prosecution, but the good faith defence will in any event apply. The good faith defence may, however, be more likely to be appropriate where a newspaper or TV or radio company runs a campaign to report alleged occurrences concerning a company which might well deny the suggestions. Even if the relevant intention could be established then it might still be possible to demonstrate good faith, eg the editor's belief in the public interest in knowing about the alleged events.

3.3   Mass trespass

The offences created in ss.6-9 Criminal Law Act 1977 are unaffected by the Act. However, s.39 introduces new powers in relation to the so-called mass trespass which was witnessed during 1985 and 1986. Where there is a refusal to leave land a power to order dispersal may exist in certain circumstances. The offences arise after such a direction has been given and there has been a failure to leave or a re-entry as a trespasser.

The new powers do not derogate from the common law remedy of self help available to occupiers, or from the powers of the police to deal with reasonably apprehended breaches of the peace; see Chapter 2. In certain instances the powers to control public assemblies may also be operative;

see s.14 (page 124), but this will be the case only where the land entered is in fact a public place under the Act.

(a) The direction to leave

The most senior police officer present at the scene (see s.39(1) and (5)) may give a direction that certain persons should leave the land in question. It is not a direction that they should not enter the land, although such a direction might properly be given under the preventive powers of the police; see *Duncan* v *Jones, Moss* v *McLachlan* and Chapter 2. The direction may be given under s.39 only if the senior police officer reasonably believes that:

- two or more persons have entered the land as trespassers *and*
- they are there with the common purpose of residing there for any period; *and*
- reasonable steps have been taken by or on behalf of the occupier to ask them to leave *and*
- *either*
  - any of those persons who entered as trespassers has caused damage to property on the land; or
  - any of those persons has used threatening, abusive or insulting words or behaviour towards the occupier, his family, employees or agent
  or
  - they have brought 12 or more vehicles onto the land (for the meaning of "vehicle" see s.39(5)).

(b) Comment

The section is not without its difficulties, although these are ultimately likely to turn upon the facts of particular cases. For definitions, see s.39(5). The direction need not be in writing and may be oral, eg by loud hailer. In the light of the requirement of *mens rea* in s.39(2) reminders of the fact of the direction may be given at appropriate times, eg before arrest.

Entry as trespasser

There need only be, for the purposes of the direction or arrest (s.39(1), (3)), a reasonable belief that there has been entry (or re-entry) as a trespasser. But for the purposes of the offence, there is a defence that the entry was not as a trespasser. It should also be noted that for the purposes of the offence the second entry need not be accompanied by an intention to reside. The Act is not intended to deal with those who enter land with permission and who outstay their welcome. Entry as a trespasser may include occasions on which entry is obtained by deceit; whether this will extend to cases where there is deception as to the length of the likely stay is uncertain. In addition, difficulties may arise if there is a claim of right to enter and remain on land. But, since these points will usually be taken after arrest and dispersal, and since they may not affect the reasonable belief of the police officer, they may be expected to arise infrequently and possibly only on the issue of the defence in s.39(4). However, where there is an apparently plausible claim of right, the police may be reluctant to intervene in what they might regard as a private matter. The conduct envisaged as a trigger to s.39 may of course give rise to separate offences, eg criminal damage or offences contrary to s.4 or s.5 of the Act.

"Reside"

This has not been defined or limited. An intention to stay for one night only will suffice. A stop-over for lunch or shopping would not amount to residing. A reasonable belief as to the common purpose will suffice.

"Land"

See s.39(5). At a late stage the Bill was amended to include agricultural buildings within the meaning of the General Rate Act 1967. The Interpretation Act 1978 also contains a definition of land which applies to the Act subject to s.39(5). Buildings other than agricultural buildings are not included in the Act.

The importance of identifying what is meant by "enters land" arises from the issue of entry to land as a trespasser, for the purposes of the direction, and, more importantly, from the nature of the offence in s.39(2), ie failing to leave or re-entering land. The identity of the land in each case becomes crucial. For example, suppose a farmer gives permission for a group of travellers to stay in one field, but, when that permission is revoked, they decamp into the farmer's adjacent field. Have they entered separate land (the adjacent field) as trespassers, or have they remained on the land (the farm as a whole)? Suppose they damage property in the adjacent field, will this be damage to property "on the land"? Suppose that the land covers a huge area, eg a forest. In such a case will "the land" mean the entire forest or simply that part into which they entered and upon which they camped? Suppose again that the farm comprises many distinct pieces of land separated by a few miles, will the whole farm be treated as the land, so that entry into one distinct piece after a direction has been given in respect of another will be entry to the same land? Suppose also that there is one owner of a huge range of properties on a country or county-wide basis, eg the Forestry Commission, the National Trust, the Crown. It might be stretching the application of the words to encompass the entire property holding and thereby to grant what would amount to a three month injunction (ie the period during which re-entry is prohibited).

"Causing damage to property on land"

"Property" is defined by reference to the Criminal Damage Act 1971 s.10 and therefore includes growing crops, trees grown for timber or fruit production, but excludes "mushrooms growing wild, flowers, fruit, foliage of a plant growing wild". Where there is damage to property on the land by the trespassers then a direction may be given. This seems to include accidental as well as deliberate damage. The property need not belong to the occupier, but would it be enough if it was damage to the property of the trespassers themselves? It is not enough for the damage to be caused to property adjacent to the land, eg if a site adjacent to a military

45

base (but not part of the highway) is occupied and the fence to the establishment is damaged.

Growing crops may be within the scope of "property" (eg in *Gayford* v *Chouler* injury to long pasture grass was damage to property within the Malicious Injury to Property Act 1861). The property must be on the land; does this include property in the land to a small degree, eg seeds? Would it be enough if there was damage to property within the land, eg pipes or conduits? Finally, will it be sufficient if there is damage to the land itself, eg by the deposit of rubbish, by churning up the surface? All these matters may involve the owner in the expense of time and money in returning the land to its former state.

In *Queen* v *Henderson & Battley* (unreported but discussed in *Cox* v *Riley*), the Court of Appeal Criminal Division decided that a development site had been damaged by the deposit on it of thirty lorry-loads of soil and rubble which cost £2,000 to remove. Mr Justice Cantley remarked that:

"Damage can be of various kinds. In the Concise Oxford Dictionary 'damage' is defined as 'injury impairing value or usefulness'. That is a definition which would fit very well with doing something to a cleared building site which at any rate for the time being impairs its usefulness as such. In addition, as it necessitates work and the expenditure of a large sum of money to restore it to its former state, it reduces its present value as a building site."

Providing damage is at least appreciable and capable of being called damage (see *Eley* v *Lytle*, *R* v *Fancy* and *A* v *Queen*) it will fall within the Act.

"Threatening", "abusive", "insulting"

See Chapter 5 for the meaning of these words.

(c) The offence

A person commits an offence if:

(i) he knows that a direction under s.39(1) has been given and that it applies to him; and
(ii) either -
   • he fails to leave the land as soon as reasonably practicable; or
   • having left the land he again enters it as a trespasser within three months from the day of the direction.

The re-entry must be as a trespasser, but need not on the face of the Act be accompanied by any purpose of residing on the land.

What will be reasonably practicable will be a matter of fact; no doubt it will include time to pack up belongings and conduct minor repairs to vehicles. It may not be an excuse that there is no petrol or that the vehicles are in need of more extensive repair. Equally, it is not enough to say that the trespassers could simply walk off the site and that by not doing so there is a failure to leave the land. May a person be treated as failing to leave the site if his vehicle is still there when it might have been driven away, or if he has left property on the site, eg a vehicle or caravan which he prefers not to take with him or cannot take with him? It would seem that a temporary and brief leaving of the site followed by a return should not fall within the Act, eg where a vehicle has been pushed from the site, or where children have been escorted to a waiting bus.

See also the discussion as to the meaning of "land" at page 44 above. Entry to a different part of the occupier's land may amount to an offence, but need the trespasser know it is the land of the same occupier?

(d) Defences in s.39(4)

Two specific defences are provided in s.39(4). The

defendant may be able to show that the original entry was not as a trespasser.

Since the arrest and direction powers are exerciseable upon reasonable suspicion that the person is a trespasser, this defence will not be available where the defendant is charged with wilful obstruction or assault of a constable in the execution of his duty. It may also be possible for the defendant to show that he has a reasonable excuse for failing to leave the land as soon as reasonably practicable or for again entering the land as a trespasser. It may be a reasonable excuse to re-enter for the purposes of recovering an abandoned vehicle or other property, eg if a person refused to leave and was arrested and he did not remove his vehicle.

The burden of proof is upon the defendant in both instances.

(e) Arrest

The power of arrest is vested in a constable in uniform (for the meaning of "uniform" see page 132 post) and is exerciseable upon reasonable suspicion that a person is committing an offence under s.39(2). The provisions of the Police and Criminal Evidence Act 1984 apply to the arrest.

3.4   Football matches

There are three areas directly affected by the Act and Sch. 1:

   (a) alcohol related offences; and
   (b) licensing; and
   (c) magistrates' powers.

(a) and (b) are affected by s.40 and Sch. 1 which make radical changes to the Sporting Events (Control of Alcohol etc) Act 1985. For the sports grounds affected see Sports Grounds and Sporting Events (Designation) Order 1985 SI 1985 No 1151.

(a) Alcohol in vehicles

Although the offences in s.1 of the Sporting Events (Control of Alcohol etc) Act 1985 were originally restricted to trains and coaches being used to take fans to football matches, the scope of that Act is now extended by the creation in Sch. 1 of s.1A to the Sporting Events (Control of Alcohol etc) Act 1985. Section 1A applies to any motor vehicle which is not a public service vehicle but which is adapted to carry more than 8 passengers and is being so used to carry 2 or more passengers on a journey to or from a designated sporting event. Section 1A makes it an offence:

(1) being within a category in s.1A(2)(a) or (b), knowingly to cause or permit intoxicating liquor to be carried in such a vehicle (s.1A(2)); or

(2) to be in possession of intoxicating liquor when in such a vehicle (s.1A(3)); or

(3) to be drunk in such a vehicle (s.1A(4)).

"Cause", "permit" and "possession" will bear their usual meanings.

Section 7(3) of that Act is also amended to extend the power of stop-search to vehicles which fall within s.1A. Section 2 of that Act also created offences which could be committed whilst at, or trying to enter, a designated sports ground. These offences are:

(1) possession of intoxicating liquor;

(2) possession of an article which is capable of causing injury to a person struck by it and which is a bottle, can, portable container used to hold drink and which is usually discarded; and

(3) being drunk.

Schedule 1 para. 1 creates s.2A which makes it an offence to possess in these circumstances certain other articles whose main purpose is the emission of a flare or smoke or visible gas or which is a firework (see s.2A(1)-(4)).

The powers to enter sports grounds to search and arrest a person reasonably suspected of an offence, should be noted (see s.7(1) and (2) of the 1985 Act).

(b) Licensing

The Sporting Events (Control of Alcohol etc) Act 1985 makes provision for regulating the supply or sale of intoxicating liquor and for the closure of bars. Schedule 1 para. 4 creates four new sections - ss. 5A, 5B, 5C and 5D in that Act. These sections make detailed changes to the licensing provisions applicable to designated sports grounds. There is a minor change to the arrangements for those rooms from which a match is visible and from which the general public is excluded. It is unlikely that police policy of objecting to the grant of special orders of exemption will cease, and the consumption of alcohol in such places will continue to be prohibited during the match itself and for a short period before and after.

(c) Exclusion orders (ss.30-37)

Magistrates' courts and Crown Courts now have power to make orders known as exclusion orders and, in conjunction with such an order, a further order that a convicted person should be photographed by the police. Procedures under this power may be likened to the procedures under the Licensed Premises (Exclusion of Certain Persons) Act 1980. Exclusion orders may only be imposed pursuant to conviction for offences defined by reference to the circumstances in which they were committed. An exclusion order prohibits the person subject to it from entering premises for the purposes of attending a prescribed football match (for the meaning of this expression see s.36) . There is also provision in s.37 for ss.30-36 to apply to other sporting events and to be modified accordingly.

The criteria for making an exclusion order

The overriding criterion for imposing an exclusion order is that the court must be satisfied that making the order would help prevent violence or disorder at or in connection with prescribed football matches (s.30(2)). Further, the defendant must have been convicted of an offence falling within at least one of the following three conditions (s.30(1)) and the order must be in addition to a sentence imposed for such an offence or in addition to a probation order or an absolute or conditional discharge (s.30(3)):

- first, an offence committed during a period relevant to a prescribed football match (see s.31(6), (7), (8) for the meaning of "relevant period") whilst the defendant was at, entering or leaving, or attempting to leave the ground. Any offence will be sufficient, eg criminal damage, assault. Offences of dishonesty are apparently included;

- secondly, an offence which:

  (i) involves the use or threat of violence by the defendant towards another person while either of them was on a journey to or from an association football match, eg where there is an "ambush" of visiting fans (s.31(3)(a)). Note that any association football match will suffice for this section; it need not be a prescribed football match. "Association football match" is not defined. Section 31(5) extends the meaning of "journey" to include breaks, even overnight breaks. "Violence" is not defined for the purposes of this part of the Act but there is no reason why it should receive a different interpretation to that given in s.8, and see also page 57. An assault would suffice, as might criminal damage caused by bricks hurled at coaches. An offence under s.4 will usually fall within this category provided that the victim was put in fear of violence being inflicted by the defendant himself. Where the offence involves the provocation of violence, other than by threatening conduct, then the category may not be satisfied; *or*

  (ii) involves the use or threat of violence towards

property and was committed by a defendant who was on a journey to or from an association football match (s.31(3)(b)); *or*

(iii)was committed by the defendant under s.5 (see page 89) or Part III of the Act (see page 102) while the defendant was on a journey to or from an association football match (s.31(3)(c)).

• Thirdly, an offence committed under s.1(3), (4) or s.1A (3), (4) of the Sporting Events (Control of Alcohol etc) Act 1985 (s.31(4)).

Factual difficulties as to the meaning of "journey" may well be common. For example, a group of youths may agree to meet at a shopping centre or public house during the morning preceding a match. At what stage can it be said that the journey of each commences? Will it be at the moment each leaves his house, or other place, intending to go to the rendez-vous; or will it be when as a group they leave the shopping centre or public house and begin to make their way to the ground?

As far as racist chanting is concerned, racist chanting by people in or trying to enter a ground will fall within the first condition; racially abusive gestures or behaviour outside a ground will fall within the second condition.

Procedures

The court will presumably indicate that it intends to make such an order. It will then invite representations from the prosecution and allow the defendant to make representations. Where the facts have not been canvassed or are otherwise not accepted by the defendant (eg after a guilty plea), it may be necessary to hear evidence on important issues, eg the extent of the journey. The requirement in s.30(2) is the overriding criterion of which the court must be satisfied. The requirement that the court should be satisfied is not a requirement for the matter to be proved on any basis other than the court asking itself "are we satisfied?". When an order has been made then the clerk or appropriate officer in the Crown Court should:

(i) give a copy to the defendant;
(ii) send a copy to the Chief Officer of Police; and
(iii) send a copy to any person prescribed by the Secretary of State
(s.34(1)).

The order will come into operation when announced in court. Its operation will not be prejudiced by non-delivery to the defendant (cf *Walsh* v *Barlow* - community service order operative even though not served).

Effect of the order and arrest (s.32)

The order prohibits the defendant from entering any premises for the purposes of attending any prescribed football match (s.30(1)). The order may be made for any period of at least three months (or for three months plus the unexpired period of any other order still extant) (s.32(1), (2)).

What is not clear is whether the order can specify only one premises (eg the ground of a particular club) or more than one (eg the clubs or grounds within a specific city). It may be possible to make a general order excluding a person from entering all premises for the purpose of attending association football matches, or to define the premises as the grounds of any club which is a member of, or is affiliated to, the football league.

A person who enters premises in breach of the order commits an offence (s.32(3)). A constable in uniform or not may arrest without warrant any person he reasonably suspects has entered premises in breach of the order. He has no power to arrest someone he reasonably suspects is about to commit an offence although entry could be denied by the club or by the constable if he anticipates a breach of the peace.

Where a person has entered premises in breach of an order (or where a constable reasonably suspects that he has done so) but he is no longer on the premises, there may be some doubt as to whether the power of arrest attaches. For example, that person may have been identified from a video film of an event or may have been identified by police officers as he was leaving the ground, or he may even have fled from police officers as they were trying to arrest him. It may be said that s.32(4) should not be read as being restricted to meaning "where a person has entered and is still on premises in breach of an order". However, the mischief is the threat which that person poses to that particular event. When he is no longer on the premises there is no longer the threat which justifies arrest, especially when the power under s.25 Police and Criminal Evidence Act 1984 is available. If a balance has to be drawn between the efficacy of policing and freedom of an individual then on this occasion the balance may lie with restricting the power to an arrest where the individual is actually on the premises, or perhaps where he is pursued from the premises (but see *Wills* v *Bowley*).

(d) Photographs

Section 35 provides that the court which makes an exclusion order may, on the application of the prosecutor, make an order requiring the person to whom it relates to attend a police station within seven days to have his photograph taken. The court may allow representations from the defence in response to the application of the prosecution. To this extent the procedure may resemble the procedure under s.49 Magistrates' Courts Act 1980 (the former power to order fingerprints to be taken) and an order in similar form would appear to be appropriate.

It is likely that in many instances a defendant will have been photographed at the police station at which he has been charged and that no application need be made. There appears to be nothing to preclude the making of an application on an occasion other than the time of conviction. Whether such an order ought to be made without the defendant being present is unclear, but it would be desirable that he be given an opportunity to make representations. There are no provisions for service of a copy of the order upon the defendant. A separate order should be made although this might be incorporated into the exclusion order. The absence of a provision for service of the order might suggest that an order ought not to be made in the absence of the defendant, unless he has been afforded an opportunity to appear.

A constable may arrest without warrant any person who fails to comply with the order and may take him to have his photograph taken. Arrest is for no other purpose, and in failing to comply with the order no offence under the Act is committed (but does such a failure amount to wilful obstruction of a constable in the execution of his duty?) The constable is not protected if he arrests a defendant who has in fact complied with the order, even if the constable has acted on reasonable suspicion.

Several provisions in the Police and Criminal Evidence Act 1984 appear to apply to arrest under s.35, although it is not an arrest for an offence. A person arrested under s.35 is not in police detention for the purposes of the 1984 Act (see s.118 of the 1984 Act). Arrest under s.35 is akin to the power in the 1984 Act to arrest for breach of a requirement to attend a police station in order to be fingerprinted. Section 28 (information to be given on arrest) and s.32(1), (2)(a) (search upon arrest) of the 1984 Act appear to apply to arrest under s.35 of the Act. The detention provisions (ss.34, 37-46) do not apply and neither does s.30 (duty to take to a police station) because there has not been an arrest for an offence. However, the common law will apply and the arrested person should be dealt with reasonably by taking him to a police station without delay for the photograph to be taken. Sections 54 (duty of custody officer to record details of possessions), 56 and 58 (right to have someone informed of arrest and access to legal advice) appear to apply to arrest under s.35.

One area of doubt is the use of force either to arrest under s.35, or to conduct the photographic session. Merely photographing a person is not a trespass, but restraining him or compelling him to remain to have a photograph taken would amount to a trespass and would take the officers beyond the execution of their duty in the absence of a power to use force. There is no express provision for the use of force in either case. Section 3 of the Criminal Law Act 1967 will only apply if it can be said that there is the arrest of "an offender" or that the person subject to the order is "unlawfully at large". Neither of these conditions is really fulfilled. The better view may be that the use of reasonable force for both purposes will be implied since to do otherwise would render the section defective and potentially meaningless.

The Act refers to "a photograph" and "his photograph". It does not say "to be photographed". Strictly construed this may mean that only one photograph may be taken without the consent of the individual. In common parlance however the phrase may mean no more than "be photographed". A photograph may mean a photograph which is not blurred or otherwise defective. Deliberately making it more difficult to take a photograph will amount to an offence contrary to s.51(3) Police Act 1964.

(e) Termination of exclusion order (s.33)

There is only one way to obtain the termination of an exclusion order. If the order was made by a magistrates' court any magistrates' court in the same petty sessional division as the court which made the order may terminate the order. In the case of an order made by the Crown Court, the same Crown Court must terminate the order. An order may only be terminated if at least one year has elapsed since the making of the order (s.33(1)). Regard must be had to the applicant's character, his conduct, the offence and other circumstances (s.33(2)). Costs may be ordered to be paid by the applicant irrespective of the success or failure of the application. If the application is refused then no further application may be entertained within the next six months (s.33(3)). The order to terminate the exclusion order must specify the date from which the exclusion order will cease to have effect. Section 34(2) prescribes the information which must be given upon termination and to whom it must be given.

Chapter 4

Riot, violent disorder and affray

4.1 Introduction

Riot (s.1), violent disorder (s.2) and affray (s.3) are the replacements for the common law offences of riot, rout, unlawful assembly and affray, which have all been abolished by s.9(1). The Act does not rely upon the concept of breach of the peace. Unlawful violence is the element common to the three major public order offences and it is appropriate to consider this in detail first. Any conduct which amounts to violence will also amount to a breach of the peace, see *R* v *Howell* , page 27.

4.2 "Violence"

"Violence" is defined in s.8 of the Act as:

"any violent conduct, so that -
(a) except in the context of affray, it includes violent conduct towards property as well as violent conduct towards persons, and
(b) it is not restricted to conduct causing or intended to cause injury or damage but includes any other violent conduct (for example, throwing at or towards a person a missile of a kind capable of causing injury which does not hit or falls short)."

Violence is a concept which is common to riot, violent disorder and affray (also to s.4, conduct intended or likely to cause fear of or provoke violence). The partial explanation in s.8 is not entirely satisfactory since it includes the word it is trying to explain. The Law Commission wanted to avoid a definition based upon specific offences against the person or property. Where such offences are committed then they may properly be charged, although in many instances of disorder it may be difficult to prove the requisite intent of the individual, the result of his action or the identity of the victim. Accordingly the Law Commission observed at para. 5.33 of their report:

"The definition ..... emphasizes the nature of violent conduct rather than its consequences ..... [V]iolence is not limited to physical damage or injury ..... and ..... it must in some way be violence towards persons or property; and the example is given of the throwing of a missile towards a person, capable of causing injury (a paper dart would thus not qualify) whether that missile falls short or wide of the mark. Many other examples of violence will amount to violent conduct upon these criteria, such as the wielding of a lethal instrument or the discharge of a firearm in the direction of another. The example is given because it explains the concept without the difficulties of a detailed list or extended definition. The conduct must be such that it can be regarded as violence towards persons or property and the jury must be sure that it was of such a character."

The definition in the Act is that of the Law Commission. Statutory definitions of violence elsewhere are rare although since "violence" is an ordinary word of the English language it will be interpreted in such a way as to be given its ordinary meaning: see *Brutus* v *Cozens*. Support for this approach will be found in *R* v *Criminal Injuries Compensation Board ex parte Warner, Webb and Others*. In deciding whether a crime was a "crime of violence" for the purposes of the scheme the court imposed no special construction; since the words were ordinary words it took the view that "the ordinary or generally understood meaning of the words must prevail". This approach was approved by the Court of Appeal in that case.

In the Law Commission Report No 76 (Conspiracy and Criminal Law Reform) it was said that "violence will cover any application of force to the person, but carries a somewhat restricted meaning in relation to property." In relation to s.2(6) Criminal Law Act 1967, force, in the context of entry to premises, was said to be the application of energy to an object with a view to moving it: *Swales* v *Cox*. Violence would suggest a higher degree of force whether applied to the person or property.

As the Law Commission explained, it would be wrong to restrict violence to cases where force is actually applied, a punch thrown which misses its target is just as much violence as a punch which finds its target. Waving a weapon so as to cause a person fear of injury or concern may properly be described as violent conduct; see s.8: " ..... it is not restricted to conduct ..... intended to cause injury .....".

It is not clear whether verbal threats alone can fall within the meaning of "violence". Whilst it may be argued that threats which are simply verbal fall within the meaning of violence, and therefore a person who issues threats of violence uses violence, the distinction in ss.1, 2 and 3 between those who threaten violence and those who use violence would militate against this view. A purely verbal threat, unaccompanied by any other activity, is unlikely to fall within the meaning of violence. In order to avoid any doubt each of s.1, s.2 and s.3 refers to the use or threat of violence. For the purposes of "affray" threats by words alone cannot amount to the offence (s.3(3)). In violent disorder both those who threaten violence and those who use violence are guilty (s.2(1)); in riot only those who use violence are guilty (s.1(1)), those who threaten violence are not guilty, except perhaps of incitement or as secondary parties. In riot those who threaten violence, whether by verbal or other means, are included when assessing the required number of participants. Any distinction between threats and actual violence may therefore be of importance only insofar as riot is concerned.

In any event, threats of any description may be dealt with under s.4 (see Chapter 5).

Whether, in the context of mass picketing or a disturbance

during a march or assembly, large numbers alone may constitute a threat of violence is not clear, although it does seem unlikely.

During the early stages of the Bill the definition of violence included "violence not justified by law, for example, the law relating to self defence or the prevention of crime or disorder". At a late stage the epithet "unlawful" was adopted in ss.1, 2, 3 (and 4) and the definition outlined above was omitted.

The use of violence for lawful purposes will not be an offence under ss.1, 2, 3 & 4. Thus violence used in self defence, or the protection of family, friends or other people, or of property, will be outside the scope of the Act provided that its use accords with the usual principles. Any person may use reasonable force in the prevention of crime, or in arresting or assisting in the arrest of an offender or suspected offender: see Criminal Law Act 1967 s.3(1) (it could be argued that the use of the word "force" in s.3 might suggest that "violence" should be read as only extending to unreasonable force, but this view would fail to give sufficient weight to the epithet "unlawful"). Violence may be used in the prevention of actual or apprehended breaches of the peace. On other occasions violence may be justified by way of self-help, eg the removal of demonstrators from a site, or trespassers from property; see the *CEGB* case, page 29. Self-help may be used to bring to an end or prevent an unlawful detention. There may be other examples of lawful violence, eg s.5 Criminal Damage Act provides a specific defence; duress and necessity may provide defences in appropriate cases. In all these matters reference should be made to the standard works available to the practitioner.

4.3 Riot (s.1)

The common law definition of riot was generally accepted as being reflected in the following extract from *Field* v *Receiver of the Metropolitan Police:*

"(1) number of persons three at least; (2) common

purpose; (3) execution or inception of the common purpose; (4) an attempt to help one another by force if necessary against a person who may oppose them in the execution of their common purpose; (5) force or violence ..... displayed in such a manner as to alarm at least one person of reasonable firmness and courage."

The offence was hedged about with uncertainties and was rarely used (perhaps 30 persons were charged each year between 1976 and 1983). The Act retains many of the features of the common law offence.

Section 1(1) provides:

"Where 12 or more persons who are present together use or threaten unlawful violence for a common purpose and the conduct of them (taken together) is such as would cause a person of reasonable firmness present at the scene to fear for his personal safety, each of the persons using unlawful violence for the common purpose is guilty of riot."

(a) Unlawful violence

Only a person using unlawful violence may be convicted of riot. Those who threaten unlawful violence may, in appropriate instances, be guilty of aiding and abetting or inciting riot (or be guilty of other offences under ss.2-5). It should be noted that those who use or threaten violence are counted for the purposes of establishing the required number of participants.

(b) Common purpose

There must be a purpose common among the participants. The retention of this (and its exclusion from violent disorder and affray) marks the special seriousness of behaviour committed collectively by a group. Riot is an offence "which derives its great gravity from the simple fact that the persons concerned were acting in numbers and using those numbers to achieve their purpose" (*R* v *Caird*).

Individual motives are irrelevant to the proof of the offence. Prior agreement or planning is not necessary. Common purpose may be shown by admissions of the defendant, by evidence of planning or by the circumstances as a whole, eg the object of the attack or the presence of banners; see s.1(3) - "the common purpose may be inferred from conduct". An accurate assessment of the activity upon which the defendant and others were engaged is all that need be shown. That activity may be stated as the common purpose, eg that they were attempting to prevent the police from gaining access to a particular place. In the past proof of common purpose has often proved to be a serious stumbling block to the successful prosecution of the more serious public order offences. No doubt these matters will continue to demand careful consideration before prosecutions are launched.

The common purpose will usually be an unlawful purpose but it may be a lawful purpose. What renders the purpose open to condemnation is the use of violence in order to achieve it. The purpose must be common to at least the minimum number of participants (ie 12).

(c) Twelve or more persons present together

The minimum number of persons who must be present together has been increased to 12 from 3. There is some historical significance in this figure (see the Riot Act 1714) but it is somewhat arbitrary. The large number does indicate the gravity attached to the offence.

The meaning of "present together" will be a question of fact for the jury. There must be violence, or the threat of violence, from each of the 12, although the violence or threats need not be simultaneous (s.1(2)). Where there is sporadic disorder it may be difficult to establish that there were 12 persons present together at the time violence was used or threatened. Where there is doubt as to the number of participants or whether they are present together, a charge of violent disorder would be more appropriate (provided that three could be shown to be present together), or even threatening behaviour contrary to s.4.

Where there are only 12 defendants and it is not alleged that there were any more participants then, in the unlikely event of a prosecution, the acquittal of one will inevitably lead to the acquittal of the remainder on the riot charges. Where, as is more likely, it is alleged that there were more than 12 participants then the acquittal of one defendant will not be fatal if the jury is satisfied that the overall number involved amounted to 12 or more; see *R* v *Beach & Morris*.

As far as the numbers involved are concerned, the *mens rea* of the offence is not taken into account in the computation of the 12 required (s.6(7)). The prosecution need only show the use or threat of violence by the other participants.

(d) Person of reasonable firmness present at the scene

The standard by which the violence or threats are judged is that of the person of reasonable firmness present at the scene. The violence must be of such a degree as would have put him in fear of his personal safety had he been there. It need not be shown that such a person was actually there or would have been likely to have come onto the scene (ss.1(4) and 2(3)). This is so even where the offence is committed in a private place to which the public does not have access. The degree of violence must be such as would cause such a person "present at the scene" to fear for his personal safety. Note that the word is "would" and not "might"; it is a degree of probability rather than possibility. In the past the proof of the degree of fear does not appear to have caused juries any problems. The feelings of anyone actually involved as a passive victim cannot be used as the measure of the requisite fear, although his evidence may of course help to establish the nature of the fear which would have been engendered in the hypothetical bystander.

"Present at the scene" was explained by the Law Commission (at para. 3.38):

" ..... As regards 'presence at the scene', there may be

some degree of uncertainty as to what is meant by 'presence', but we doubt whether it is possible or desirable to be more specific as to how far away from or how near to the disturbance the hypothetical person must be. Every case will to this extent depend on its circumstances, but we believe that a jury will sufficiently understand what is meant by 'present at the scene', that is anyone who would have been in real danger of becoming involved in the disturbance."

(e) Public or private place

There is no restriction on the location in which the ingredients of a riot may occur. This affirms the common law approach; see, for example, *Pitchers* v *Surrey County Council*, where the riot occurred in an army camp.

(f) Mens rea

Section 6 states the *mens rea* required for all the offences under Part I of the Act. For the purposes of riot, s.6(1) is relevant. Section 6(5) and (6) are common to all the offences. The effect of s.6(7) is that:

"when a person is charged with an offence where proof of a number of participants is required ..... the mental element ..... requires to be proved only in relation to that person: the mental element of the other participants ..... is irrelevant." (Law Commission explanatory note to the draft Bill)

It follows that the self-induced intoxication of the others is also irrelevant for the purposes of calculating the number present. However, where intoxication is alleged there may be difficulties in establishing a common purpose.

It must be shown that the defendant intended to use violence or that he was aware that his conduct may have been violent. Whilst stressing that *mens rea* is relatively unimportant from a practical point of view, the Law Commission deliberately effected a move away from the view of recklessness, as

64

applied in *R* v *Caldwell*, and preferred the approach taken in the case of *R* v *Cunningham*. The *mens rea* is therefore either an intention to do the harm, or foresight of the type of harm, and a decision to take the risk. For further discussion of the mental element in crime the reader is referred to the standard works on criminal law and to the discussion in the Law Commission report at paras. 3.41 to 3.54.

Generally, where awareness is impaired by intoxication the defendant will be taken to have been aware of that of which he would have been aware if he had not been intoxicated (s.6(5)). Where the defendant alleges that the intoxication was not self-induced or was a result of medical treatment then the burden will be upon the defendant to prove this on the balance of probabilities.

Where the defendant is so intoxicated that he cannot form the common purpose necessary then he is entitled to be acquitted since:

"the element of common purpose ..... amounts in substance to a further mental element of intent ..... [I]f there were sufficient evidence to indicate that a defendant accused of riot was too intoxicated to have the common purpose, he could not be found guilty of riot" (The Law Commission Report para. 6.28).

He could however be found guilty of violent disorder which does not rely upon any element of common purpose.

(g) Miscellaneous matters

Consent to prosecutions: Prosecutions for riot or incitement to riot must be by, or with the consent of, the DPP (s.7(1)). The practice of consent being given by the DPP's local representative (the Chief Crown prosecutor) may not be followed in this case. The consent of the Attorney General is also required for offences in relation to racial hatred. These consents are now governed by ss.25 and 26 Prosecution of Offences Act 1985. Consent need only be lodged at the court of trial with the clerk and need not be proved (see *R* v *Dexter*;

R v *Metz* and now s.25 of the 1985 Act). A consent in broad terms, eg where the charge is not specified, is nonetheless sound; see *R* v *Cain*, where the consent read:

> "In pursuance of my powers under the ..... Act I hereby consent to the prosecution of (name) of (address) for an offence or offences contrary to the provisions of the said Act."

In *R* v *Pearce* consent in the above form sufficed for a prosecution under s.5A of the 1936 Act but it did not provide consent to prosecution for conspiracy to commit s.5A offences since it did not refer to any Act but the 1936 Act (as amended).

Arrest: Riot is an arrestable offence (by virtue of the possible term of imprisonment) and the provisions of the Police and Criminal Evidence Act 1984 apply; see especially s.24 (arrest without warrant on reasonable suspicion of committing or having committed an arrestable offence) and s.28 (statement of reasons). A statement that arrest is for rioting may be preferable, but an indication that the arrest is for using violence may suffice since it indicates the nature of the offence. In any event, the power at common law to arrest for breach of the peace exists and a statement that the arrest is for breach of the peace would serve for the time being, although a full statement of reasons and arrest on the charge of riot would have to follow in accordance with the Act.

Trial: The offence is triable only on indictment. The maximum sentence is ten years' imprisonment or a fine or both (s.1(6)).

Duplicity: Section 1 is to be treated as creating one offence only; see s.7(2).

Dispersal of rioters: The powers and duties to disperse rioters have already been dealt with; see breach of the peace powers, Chapter 2.

Riot by involvement in other offences: In *R* v *Sharp* &

Johnson Lord Goddard remarked that:

"The term riot is a term of art and, contrary to popular belief, a riot may involve no noise or disturbance of the neighbours though there must be some force or violence. For instance, if three men enter a shop and forcibly or by threats steal goods therein technically they are guilty not only of larceny or robbery but also of riot."

See also *Dwyer* v *Receiver of the Metropolitan Police*, a case on the Riot (Damages) Act 1886, where four hooded men armed with iron bars raided a jeweller's shop and robbed the owner; it was held that there had been a riot. Under the terms of the Act, provided there are sufficient participants, there is no reason why this result should not follow, eg a large gang raid on a warehouse or security van. Violent disorder might also be charged, but with a relatively low maximum penalty this may not be appropriate.

Aid; abet; incite: Mere presence at the scene will not suffice; there must be a sufficient degree of participation or active encouragement (for an extreme example see *Devlin* v *Armstrong*) or promotion by words, signs or other actions. The general law of aiding and abetting and incitement applies and the reader is referred to the standard texts upon the subject, and to *Allen & Others* v *Ireland*.

(h) Riot in other legislation (s.10)

Riot and cognate expressions occur in numerous statutes. The effect of s.10 is clear with regard to the Acts specified, ie the Riot (Damages) Act 1886, Merchant Shipping Act 1894, Marine Insurance Act 1906. Thus in the first two Acts the words "riotous" and "riotously" will be construed in accordance with s.1. In the third Act, policies will be construed in accordance with s.1 unless the contrary intention appears. In marine insurance policies the word "riot" bears the meaning given to it by the common law so that the provisions of s.1 are now appropriate; see *The Andreas Lemos* where Staughten J construed the word "riot" in a policy according to the common law. Thus a clandestine theft was not a riot: "Nobody but a Sloane Ranger would say ..... 'it was a riot'."

The effect on other legislation is less clear. It appears that most legislation is construed in accordance with the common law view of riot and will therefore now be interpreted in the light of s.1. Examples would be the Licensing Act 1964, the Representation of the People Act 1983, and the Ecclesiastical Courts Jurisdiction Act 1860.

The Riot (Damages) Act 1886 deserves some attention since it provides a scheme for compensation in respect of damage to property flowing from riots. For personal injury a claim might be made under the Criminal Injuries Compensation scheme. The 1886 Act replaced earlier Acts which had themselves consolidated and amended the laws relating to remedies against "the hundred". The Act deals only with injury to property, ie "house, shop or building" and property therein; motor cars in the street would not be within the scope of the Act. The assembly must not only be riotous, but also tumultuous. A crime of stealth will not be covered; see *Dwyer* v *Receiver of the Metropolitan Police*. There must be rioters who are "in such numbers and in such a state of agitated commotion and ..... generally so acting, that the forces of law and order should have been well aware of the threat which existed .....".

The Act provides for a form of contributory negligence; where the applicant provoked or contributed to the riot or to his own loss, the compensation may be reduced. The procedures for claim are governed by regulation (see Riot (Damages) (Amendment) Regulations 1986, SI 1986 No 36), and the claim will be made to the relevant police authority (the Receiver in the Metropolitan Police District).

4.4 Violent disorder (s.2)

Violent disorder is the successor to the common law offence of unlawful assembly. This was generally regarded as being made out where there was "an assembly of three or more persons with a common purpose either to commit a crime of violence or to achieve any other object, lawful or not, in such a way as to cause a reasonable man to apprehend a breach of the peace."

When considering the replacement of unlawful assembly, the government chose not to follow the recommendation of the Law Commission for the creation of two offences, one of which (using violence) would be triable on indictment, the other of which (threatening violence) would be triable summarily. Under the Act both those who use and those who threaten unlawful violence may be tried for the same offence, and jointly. It is upon sentence that distinctions may be drawn between levels and manner of involvement.

(a) The elements of violent disorder (s.2(1))

Section 2(1) of the Act provides:

"Where 3 or more persons who are present together use or threaten unlawful violence and the conduct of them (taken together) is such as would cause a person of reasonable firmness present at the scene to fear for his personal safety, each of the persons using or threatening unlawful violence is guilty of violent disorder."

The new offence differs from the common law in one important respect; it lacks the element of common purpose. It relies on the fear of an individual for his personal safety where that fear is induced by actual use or threats of violence. An assembly of individuals who intend either to commit a crime by open force or to further a common purpose by methods which could cause apprehension of breaches of the peace, will not commit an offence of violent disorder. Previously such an assembly would have been an unlawful assembly. This may be of importance where there is evidence of an assembly at which is planned a series of attacks on different targets one after another. Whether or not the participants are prevented from carrying out any or all of these attacks, the initial assembly will not constitute the offence of violent disorder, but each attack may.

(b) At least three persons

There must be at least 3 persons present together. There is no need to establish a common purpose, although it must be possible to say that the participants were "present together". This seems to be a requirement of at least knowledge of each other's presence, but it is not a requirement that they should have a common purpose or that they should be acting in concert. In most cases there will be no difficulty in establishing that the participants are present together, eg a gang of youths on a street corner hurling missiles at a police car or bus. In some cases the facts may not allow of such easy interpretation, eg sporadic violence or threats from a few people in a large crowd. In such instances charges of threatening behaviour contrary to s.4 would be appropriate, or, in extreme instances, affray contrary to s.3.

The use or threat of violence need not be simultaneous (s.2(2)) but there must presumably be something more than sporadic or infrequent acts or threats of violence; these are unlikely to generate the degree of fear necessary to establish the offence.

Unlike riot, both those who threaten and those who use unlawful violence are guilty of violent disorder.

(c) Unlawful violence: See page 57.

(d) Bystander: See page 63.

(e) Private or public places

As with riot and affray, the offence may be committed in either a public or a private place (s.2(4)), eg in a public house, on a road, or at a private party. There is no reason why the offence should not be committed in a dwelling-house. It should be noted that offences contrary to ss.4 and 5 do not normally extend to conduct occurring in a dwelling-house.

(f) Mens rea

The *mens rea* requirement is to be found in s.6(2); see also s.6(5), (6) and (7) (see page 64).

(g) Continuing offence

Unlawful assembly was a continuing offence and the offending activity might be one event or a series of acts taking place over different locations, provided always that the common purpose was not lost. In *R* v *Jones* it was suggested that a count in an indictment disclosed more than one offence since it, and further particulars, referred to several sites at which similar incidents of violence occurred on the same day. The defence suggested that the incidents at each site were isolated and separated from each other by journeys and meal breaks during which no violence took place. The court rejected this:

"..... The ingredients of the offence are (i) the *actus reus* of coming together and (ii) the *mens rea* involved in the intention of fulfilling a common purpose in such a manner as to endanger the public peace. These ingredients have to be co-existent. There is nothing ..... which indicates that, at any time between the arrival at Shrewsbury and the departure from Telford, those charged with the offence ceased to be an assembly or ceased to have the intent of making an unlawful assembly."

It is submitted that, with the relaxation of the common law requirement of assembly for a common purpose, a different conclusion would now be reached. If this is so, separate counts for each incident will have to be preferred in cases like *R* v *Jones*. Each of the incidents would be separated by a substantial period of inactivity during which no bystander would be put in fear.

(h) Arrest

Violent disorder is an arrestable offence by virtue of the possible sentence (see s.2(5)), and the power to arrest without warrant under s.24 Police and Criminal Evidence Act 1984 applies. The appropriate statement of reasons should refer to violent disorder although it may be that the use of the word "violence" would adequately indicate to the defendant the reasons for the arrest. Since the offence contains the elements of a breach of the peace, an arrest or other preventive action made in that respect would be permissible.

(i) Duplicity

Although s.2 may be read as creating two offences, s.7(2) provides that for relevant purposes it is to be treated as creating one offence only.

(j) Trial

Violent disorder is triable on indictment (maximum of five years imprisonment) or summarily (maximum six months imprisonment or a fine or both) (s.2(5)). A person tried on indictment may, if found not guilty, be found guilty of an offence under s.4 (s.7(3)) and may be punished accordingly (s.7(4)). Section 6(3) of the Criminal Law Act 1967, which also allows for alternative verdicts, is unaffected by s.7.

(k) Policy behind s.2

Both the Law Commission and the government in its White Paper indicated their view of prosecution policy and in the light of the large degree of overlap between the offences in ss.2 - 5 the comments are of interest:

"Of course, not every case in which three or more people participate in the specified conduct will necessarily be regarded as appropriate to be dealt with under this offence. Prosecutors may well feel that some cases are not sufficiently serious to warrant proceedings for a 'combination' offence and that this offence will be appropriate for use only when the extra gravity of the circumstances of the group's conduct is such as to justify prosecution for such an offence." (Law Commission, para. 5.29).

"Like the Law Commission, the government anticipates that it [violent disorder] will be used in the future as the normal charge for serious outbreaks of public disorder. But it will be capable of being applied over a wide spectrum of situations ranging from major public disorder to minor group disturbances involving some violence. The proposal to make it triable either way will give it a useful degree of flexibility for dealing with lesser outbreaks of group violence, such as those commonly associated with football hooliganism." (White Paper, para.3.13)

4.5 Affray

(a) Introduction

The common law offence of affray consisted of unlawful fighting or display of force in such a manner that a person of reasonably firm character might be likely to be terrified. Although the offence had fallen into disuse it enjoyed a rejuvenation in the 1950s. The Law Commission observed:

"Affray is typically charged in cases of pitched street battles between rival gangs, spontaneous fights in public houses, clubs and at seaside resorts, and revenge attacks on individuals. It is sometimes charged on its own, but is often accompanied by charges of one or more other offences, most of them falling within the general rubric of offences against the person."

The higher courts emphasized that there should be a high degree of fear and that this requirement should not be watered down The retention of an offence of affray which reflects much of the common law, marks the seriousness of the offence, not so much for the extent of the injuries inflicted but rather because of the nature of the offence, ie the participation in acts of violence causing alarm and terror to the public. It is essentially an offence against public order not an offence against the person. The government was able to accept the recommendations of the Law Commission and to give effect to them in the Act.

(b) The elements of affray

"A person is guilty of an affray if he uses or threatens unlawful violence towards another and his conduct is such as would cause a person of reasonable firmness present at the scene to fear for his personal safety." (s.3(1) of the Act)

(c) Unlawful violence

A person must use or threaten unlawful violence (s.3(1)). Note that the word "violence" does not include violence to property (s.8). The unlawful violence must be used or threatened "towards another"; violence offered to passers-by generally would be sufficient. There must in this sense be a victim. The phrase "towards another" is found in s.4 and it suggests that the defendant must be at least aware of the presence of the other person. The fear induced in the victim does not replace the fear of the hypothetical bystander as the gauge of the violence but will be one of those matters taken into account in assessing the likely impact upon the hypothetical bystander.

Threats of unlawful violence cannot be by words alone (s.3(3)). This reflects the view of the common law (see *R* v *Sharp &Johnson* and *Taylor* v *DPP*). The brandishing of a weapon would suffice; such conduct would also fall within ss.4 and 5 of the Act and s.1 Prevention of Crime Act 1953.

Where a group is involved, the individual will still be guilty of affray even if his own actions taken alone would not amount to an offence, eg by not causing the necessary degree of terror. It is the conduct of the group which must be considered and the terror which is induced by that conduct (s.3(2)).

(d) Private and public places

The offence may be committed in public and in private. This reflects the common law (s.3(5)).

(e) Bystander

See page 63. Neither the actual nor the likely presence of a person of reasonable firmness need be shown (s.3(4)). This confirms the approach of the common law to attacks in public places (see *Att Gen Reference No 3 of 1983*) although it is wider than the common law approach to violence in a private place where it had to be shown that a person was likely to come across the violence.

Since the offence may be committed by one person only, it would be possible to convict of affray in a wide variety of instances, eg where there was an attack by a youth on his parents in the home. Whether it would be proper to bring a charge on such an occasion is another issue. The Law Commission remarked:

> " ..... it seems unlikely ..... that a personal quarrel between two people involving mutual assaults without the danger of the involvement of others ..... would fall within the offence ..... such incidents can hardly be said to give rise to the serious disturbance to public order with which the offence is intended to deal." (para.3.38).

(f) Mens rea: See s.6(2), (5) and (6); and page 64.

(g) Arrest

Affray is not an arrestable offence since it does not fall within the criteria in s.24 Police and Criminal Evidence Act 1984. There is, however, a power for a constable to arrest without warrant (s.3(6)), which power is expressed in limited terms. It is restricted to arrest on reasonable suspicion that the person is committing the offence. Where the activity has terminated there is no power to arrest without warrant unless the provisions of s.25 Police and Cirminal Evidence Act 1984 apply, as they might well do in cases where there is a need to prevent further violence or damage. A statement of reasons using the word(s) "affray" or "violence" or "threat of violence" would be sufficient to explain the grounds for the arrest. The common law power to arrest or restrain to prevent apprehended breaches of the peace would be available (see page 31), eg, if a renewal was feared.

(h) Trial

The offence is triable either way with a maximum sentence on trial on indictment of 3 years or a fine or both (s.3(7)). In cases where the evidence is complex, where the trial may take a substantial period, where the number of defendants is large, where issues of self-defence may be raised, or where violence is extreme or premeditated or not spontaneous, then trial on indictment may be appropriate (see also *R* v *Crimlis*). In other cases summary trial may be appropriate.

The possibility of summary trial will enable the prosecution both to indicate the nature of the violence and to draw a clear distinction between that conduct and conduct within s.4. There is a large degree of overlap between s.4 and s.3 and in some instances a charge under s.3 will be appropriate. At the same time, a trial on indictment might be felt to be too heavy-handed, and yet summary trial under s.4 might not be felt to represent the alleged degree of criminality of the participants. In this instance a charge under s.3 and summary trial would be appropriate.

A person tried on indictment may, if found not guilty, be found guilty of an offence under s.4 (s.7(3)) and may be punished accordingly (s.7(4)). Section 6(3) Criminal Law Act 1967, which allows for alternative verdicts, is unaffected by s.7.

(i) Duplicity

Section 3 might be read as creating two offences. To avoid doubt or difficulties, s.7(2) provides that for relevant purposes it creates only one offence. Once the fighting ceases then the offence terminates. Should fighting recommence then a new offence starts. Should the fighting spill from one place to another without ceasing then one offence only is committed; see *R* v *Woodrow*.

Chapter 5

Threatening, abusive, insulting and disorderly conduct and racial hatred

5.1 Introduction

The redrawing of the well known offence under s.5 of the 1936 Act presented the government with its most difficult problem in terms both of drafting and policy. In s.5 of the 1936 Act Parliament had attempted to "solve the difficult question how far freedom of speech and behaviour must be limited in the general public interest" (per Lord Reid in *Brutus* v *Cozens*). The Law Commission considered s.5 of the 1936 Act in the context of its proposal for a scheme of public order offences. The detailed discussion at paras. 5.1 - 5.22 of the Law Commission's report is a valuable critique of the interpretation of s.5. In particular, the Law Commission and the government identified the following points which emerge from the case law on s.5 of the 1936 Act:

(a) the need, insofar as practicable, to maintain the principle in *Beatty* v *Gillbanks*, namely that provided a person's conduct is not threatening, abusive or insulting he will commit no offence even if it provokes others to violence;

(b) the need to avoid the use of the concept of "breach of the peace";

(c) that there were some theoretical difficulties which arose from the aspect of causation in s.5 of the 1936

Act; see especially *Parkin* v *Norman*. Part and parcel of this was the need to protect those who are disinclined to react to threatening, abusive or insulting conduct by themselves having recourse to violence. The example given by the Law Commission was of an elderly lady subjected to threatening, abusive or insulting conduct who would be unlikely to react in such manner as to occasion a breach of the peace. No s.5 offence would (in theory) have been committed (although it must be said that in practice a conviction would be likely), but the Law Commission felt that the conduct warranted the condemnation inherent in a criminal offence. Another example may be seen in *Marsh* v *Arscott* where it was said that police officers subjected to threatening, abusive or insulting conduct could not be said to be likely to react by causing a breach of the peace. Being put in fear was not of itself sufficient for the offence to be made out. Section 5 was concerned with cause and effect and the necessary effect was a breach of the peace; it was not enough that the conduct of the defendant should itself amount to a breach of the peace;

(d) the offence was restricted to public places and there was a need to avert difficulties apparently encountered at major public disorder incidents, and in some other minor cases (eg *Marsh* v *Arscott*, *R* v *Edwards & Roberts*) where the offending activity occurred on private premises to which the public did not have access;

(e) s.5 of the 1936 Act was not designed to deal with minor acts of hooliganism either falling short of the criteria of threatening, abusive or insulting, or which engendered not fear of violence but a more generalised sense of unease or apprehension.

The government rejected the Law Commission's proposals for the revision of unlawful assembly but elements of the Law Commission recommendations in that respect have been adapted in the new offences in ss.4 and 5 of the Act.

Sections 4 and 5 have been developed to rectify the deficiencies in s.5 of the 1936 Act and, although they do overlap to a large degree, the former is intended to deal with more serious misbehaviour than the latter.

The government has also taken the oppportunity to repeal s.5A of the 1936 Act and to create six separate offences in ss.18-23. Some of the deficiencies in the 1936 Act have been remedied, although the offences are still likely to prove difficult to use in practice.

5.2 Fear or provocation of violence (s.4)

Section 4(1) provides:

"A person is guilty of an offence if he -
(a) uses towards another person threatening, abusive or insulting words or behaviour, or
(b) distributes or displays to another person any writing, sign or other visible representation which is threatening, abusive or insulting
with intent to cause that person to believe that immediate unlawful violence will be used against him or another by any person, or to provoke the immediate use of unlawful violence by that person or another, or whereby that person is likely to believe that such violence will be used or it is likely that such violence will be provoked."

(a) The venue

As with the other public order offences, s.4 is not restricted to public places and the offence may, with one exception, be committed anywhere (s.4(2)). This is a major change from the position under the 1936 Act and effectively reverses decisions such as *Marsh v Arscott* (shop car park) and *R v Edwards & Roberts* (front garden of a house), where on the facts the relevant place was found not to be a public place. There is now no need to decide whether a place is a public or a private place.

The only restriction is where the conduct occurs in a dwelling (defined in s.8). Where the conduct occurs in a garden or on a driveway or on a staircase of a block of flats then the offence may be committed. Where a person inside a dwelling uses threatening, abusive or insulting conduct towards someone outside, eg in the street, at the front door or in the garden of that or another house, then the offence may be committed. The trespassing hooligan (see *R v Edwards & Roberts*) will no longer have a defence, provided he is not in a dwelling-house. A person who posts offensive literature through a letter box will be guilty of an offence since the distribution does not occur in a dwelling.

(b) What conduct is prohibited?

The prohibited conduct is the same as for s.5 of the 1936 Act, ie it consists of (a) the use of words or behaviour or (b) the distribution or display of any writing, sign or other visible representation. The display of a flag, badge, emblem, armband or "tee-shirt", may fall within s.4. "Display" and "distribute" are not defined for the purposes of s.4, although on general principles they ought to be given their ordinary meanings. "Distribute" in Part III of the Act (racial hatred) is restricted to distribution to the public or a section of the public. This qualification is omitted from s.4 and any distribution will suffice. For a discussion of "distribute" see *R v Britton*, page 106.

(c) What quality must the conduct possess?

To constitute the offence, the conduct must be threatening or abusive or insulting. These words were, of course, found in s.5 of the 1936 Act and their application is well known. There should be no use of synonymous expressions such as "behaviour evidencing a disrespect or contempt for the rights of others". Conduct which is annoying is not enough (see *Brutus v Cozens*); it must be more than disgusting or offensive behaviour (*Parkin v Norman*). The words were described in *Jordan v Burgoyne* as "very strong words". *Brutus v Cozens* is the leading case on the interpretation of the words and the House of Lords refused to attempt any definition:

"vigourous and it may be distasteful or unmannerly speech or behaviour is permitted so long as it does not go beyond any of three limits ..... They are all limits easily recognisable by the ordinary man" (per Lord Reid).

" ..... no words of definition are needed. The words ..... are clear and they convey of themselves a meaning which the ordinary citizen can well understand" (per Lord Morris)

" ..... an ordinary sensible man knows an insult when he sees one ..... Parliament has given no indication that the word is to be given any unusual meaning. Insulting means insulting and nothing else" (per Lord Reid).

There is no requirement that any person should actually feel insulted or threatened or abused. In *Parkin* v *Norman*, McCullough J remarked that:

" ..... if the conduct in question is of this character it does not in our judgment matter whether anyone feels himself to have been threatened abused or insulted. Insulting behaviour does not lose its insulting character simply because no-one who witnessed it was insulted ....." .

In *Parkin* v *Norman* itself, the activity had not and would not have been witnessed by anyone who would have been insulted; nonetheless it could be classed as "potentially insulting". That potentiality gave it the necessary character of insulting (see also *Nicholson* v *Gage*).

The approach of the court in *Brutus* v *Cozens* and *Parkin* v *Norman* are of general application and the latter has been applied to the meaning of "threatening"; see *Ewart* v *Rogers*, where the need for an element of menace in order to constitute a threat was recognised.

The judgment in *Parkin* v *Norman* also gives useful observations upon the nature of an insult, but without in any way attempting a definition. It seems that this approach can be applied equally to threats and abuse:

> "One cannot insult nothing. The word presupposes a subject and an object and, in this day and age, a human object. An insult is perceived by someone who feels insulted. It is given by someone who is directing his words or behaviour to another person or persons. When A is insulting B, and is clearly directing his words and behaviour to B alone, if C hears and sees is he insulted? He may be disgusted, offended, angered and no doubt a number of other things as well; and he may be provoked by what he sees and hears into breaking the peace. But will he be insulted? One must take care not to be too analytical or refined about these things."

This *dictum* suggests that for there to be an insult the conduct had to be directed at a specific person or persons. In *R* v *Newham JJ ex parte Sadiku*, the Divisional Court took this approach and concluded that urinating on the public highway could not be said to be "insulting" in the circumstances of that case: "There was no question here of the behaviour being in any way directed at the persons who were present." However, in *Masterson* v *Holden*, homosexual embracing in Oxford Street at 1.55 a.m. could properly be regarded as "insulting" even though not directed at any particular person or group. The court explained the *dictum* in *Parkin* v *Norman* on the basis that:

> "What the ..... passage must be understood to mean is that words or behaviour cannot be insulting if there is not a human target which they strike, whether they were intended to strike that target or not ..... The magistrates were perfectly entitled to infer that the two appellants must have known that other people would be likely to be present ..... Their conduct ..... if in the ordinary sense it was capable of being insulting, would be likely to make some impact on anybody who was nearby ..... [I]t can properly be said that the conduct could be insulting albeit it was not deliberately aimed at a particular person."

The significance of the words "directed towards" or "aimed

at" can now be seen in the opening phrase of s.4(1)(a); see page 84. This seems to resolve any residual argument as to which of the cases took the correct approach.

In practice the criteria may not have been applied strictly and the flexibility of the 1936 Act in practice is well known. Above all, the decisions indicate that the issue is one of fact and the Divisional Court will not interfere with the findings of fact unless no court properly directing itself could have reached that conclusion. But the prosecution now have available the offence under s.5 of the Act. This may be used in many instances when s.5 may have been used in the past and when its use was not altogether happy.

(d) Intention to use conduct of the appropriate character

Viscount Dilhorne in *Brutus v Cozens* said:

> "..... the justices ..... may well have concluded that the appellant's behaviour did not evince any intention to insult either players or spectators, and so could not properly be regarded as insulting."

None of their other Lordships made any observation upon this point. This view was not favoured by McCullough J in *Parkin v Norman*. He regarded intention as irrelevant: "..... threats abuse and insults are within the section whether or not they were intended to be threats abuse or insults."

The government at first preferred the approach of McCullough J, which was approved in *Masterson v Holden*, but at a later stage it introduced s.6(3) to reflect the views of the Law Commission. Section 6(3) requires the prosecution to establish not only that the conduct had the necessary character, but also that the defendant, in the circumstances in which he used the conduct, intended it to have, or was aware that it may have had, that character. In most cases proof of the intention will derive from the character of the conduct and the surrounding circumstances. An inadvertent use of what is an insult ought not to be an offence within s.4

(e)   Uses ..... towards another person

These words were not found in the 1936 Act, nor, significantly, are they to be found in s.5 of the Act. As has already been seen, the phrase is reminiscent of McCullough J's comment in *Parkin* v *Norman* that " ..... the defendant's conduct was aimed at one person and one person only". Irrespective of the conflict between *Parkin* v *Norman* and *Masterson* v *Holden*, the use of the words in s.4(1)(a) introduces a requirement that the defendant must be shown deliberately to have directed his conduct at a specific person or persons and must therefore be shown to have been aware of, or perhaps reckless as to, their presence. It must then be shown that the conduct falls within one of the three categories prescribed by the Act.

There is nothing to suggest that the conduct need be threatening, abusive or insulting to that other person (or persons), although this will usually be the case; in any event the other person need not actually feel threatened etc. The other person will usually be a victim, but this will not always be the case. Sometimes the other person will in fact be an associate of the defendant and the threats, abuse or insults will have been directed to him with a view to encouraging him to violence against another. If the intended or likely effect of the conduct is to encourage any person to indulge in violence then the offence will be made out.

Suppose on a picket line one picket uses, towards a person passing through the picket line on a bus, threatening behaviour. The picket may be convicted of a s.4 offence either because of the likelihood that the worker will believe that immediate violence will be used (eg throwing of stones, banging on the side of the bus) or because the threats are likely to provoke violence. Such violence will not be by the person towards whom the threats were made but will be by other persons present at the scene who are likely to be provoked to violence.

Nor is there anything to suggest that the conduct should be

observed by the other person, although whether or not it is
may affect the issue of likelihood of violence, eg where X
gestures aggressively towards Y who is unaware of the
gesture.

(f) Intention or likelihood/causing fear or provocation of unlawful violence

Just as s.5 of the 1936 Act was concerned with cause and
effect, so too is s.4 of the Act, ie it is concerned with conduct
which is intended or likely to cause fear or to provoke
unlawful violence. It is not concerned with conduct which is
itself violent unless that conduct is supported by the
necessary intention or likelihood. Nor is s.4 concerned with
the actual effect of the behaviour. The intended or likely
consequences are what matter.

What has to be intended to be caused or provoked (or to be
likely to be caused or provoked) is the major change to the
previous law and remedies one of the defects identified by
the government in its White Paper and by the Law
Commission. It must be shown *either* that the person at
whom the conduct had been aimed was intended, or likely, to
be made to believe that unlawful violence would be inflicted
on him or another, *or* that the person at whom the conduct
has been aimed, or someone else, was intended or likely to
be provoked to unlawful violence.

One of four alternative states of affairs must be shown:

- that the defendant intended to cause the person at
  whom he directed the conduct to believe that immediate
  unlawful violence would be used against him, or
  another person, by any person, ie by the defendant or
  anyone else; or
- that the defendant intended to provoke the person at
  whom he directed the conduct, or any other person, to
  use immediate unlawful violence; or
- that it was likely that the person at whom he directed
  the conduct would believe that immediate unlawful
  violence would be used (presumably against him or

any other person); or
- that it was likely that immediate unlawful violence by the person at whom he directed the conduct, or by any other person, would be provoked.

Although intention will frequently be inferred from the nature of the conduct, on occasions it may well be difficult to prove intention. It may be easier to prove the likelihood of the conduct either causing the other person to believe that violence will be used or provoking violence, whether on the part of that person or some other person. In neither case is there any need to demonstrate actual belief that violence would occur, or actual provocation to violence. The offence is intended to deal with threats to the peace and not actual outbreaks of violence.

The Act uses the word "likely"; ie regard must always be had to the circumstances, and likelihood is a higher burden to overcome than "liable"; see *Parkin* v *Norman*. Police officers are not "likely" to react by using unlawful violence, but they are "likely" to believe that unlawful violence will be used against them. Whether or not conduct has the necessary character is decided by the ordinary man, who may take into account the actual audience or victim or participants; it is not decided by asking whether the audience or victim felt threatened etc. But the likelihood of fear or provocation of violence can only be assessed by reference to the actual audience or victim or participants. The speaker who uses what are objectively assessed as threats etc to an audience which has special susceptibilities, even a predisposition to violence, must take that audience as he finds it. He cannot plead for his actions to be tested against a "reasonable audience"; see *Jordan* v *Burgoyne*. Nor is it possible to argue that conduct should be tested against a "reasonably firm bystander". The section is intended to protect both the public peace and the timid citizen.

The belief of the person towards whom the conduct is directed need not be reasonable; it may be entirely unreasonable or irrational. The user of such conduct must take his victim as he finds him. If, given the character of the victim, it is likely that he will fear the infliction of violence then that is an end of the matter. Indeed, as has been seen, there need not actually be such a belief; intention to cause such a belief is sufficient, as is likelihood that such belief will be caused.

In *Marsh* v *Arscott* the charge failed on two points: (i) the car park in question was not a public place; (ii) even though the behaviour may have been threatening abusive or insulting, it was not likely to occasion a breach of the peace since the only people who witnessed it were police officers. Police officers could not be said to be likely to react in that way. Under s.4 a conviction might now follow since (i) the offence can be committed on private property; and (ii) the person towards whom the conduct has been directed, the police officer, might be likely to believe that unlawful violence would be used against him.

Where the conduct is intended, or likely, to encourage persons other than the "victim" to react violently then the offence will be made out. In *Simcock* v *Rhodes* an abusive remark by one youth to a police officer was not likely to cause the police officer to react by causing a breach of the peace. However, there were present at the scene other youths and it was likely that they would be encouraged to breaches of the peace. In terms of s.4, abusive language had been used towards another person (the police officer) whereby it was likely that unlawful violence would be provoked; violence not by the police officer but by the other youths. The defendant had also used abusive language towards another person (the police officer) who was likely to believe that violence on the part of those present would be used against him. The case also demonstrates the difficulties inherent in the formulation "uses towards another person". It could be said that the language had been used towards everyone present and not simply the police officer.

(g) Immediate unlawful violence

See s.8 and page 57 for the meaning of "unlawful violence". This is a major departure from the 1936 Act and replaces the concept of breach of the peace used in that Act. The use of the word "immediate" was taken by the Law Commission in its report and Working Paper to correspond closely to the concept of "imminence" in the common law breach of the peace preventive powers (cf *Moss* v *McLachlan*). In the usual case there will be no real difficulty in establishing the immediacy of the violence. For example, where one group of football supporters aims threats or insults at an opposing group on the other side of the ground, it is easy to envisage the fear or provocation of immediate violence, eg by a reciprocation of the threats, gesticulations and attempts to attack. Equally the threat might be of post-match violence; this might still have the quality of imminence in the sense of proximate in time and space. A more difficult case might be where threats are aimed at a group, eg a religious or ethnic group who live predominantly on the opposite side of a town. That other group might be intended or likely to fear unlawful violence. It might not be easy to establish that the violence they would fear could properly be termed immediate.

One situation which would appear not to fall within the ambit of s.4 is that which arose in *R* v *Ambrose*. The appellant addressed, to a girl aged 12, words which were not found to fall within the Act as being at worst rude and offensive. The girl reported the words to her father who, together with another man, became very angry and indicated that they felt like assaulting the appellant. Because of the finding on the language the court felt that there was no need to enquire further into the question whether insulting words are likely to cause a breach of the peace if the breach of the peace is likely to occur some time later and in different circumstances. In this sort of case, where the victim is not likely or intended to be caused to fear the infliction of violence, no offence will be made out since the violence likely to be provoked could not be described as immediate.

(h) Arrest

There is a power for a constable, in uniform or not, to arrest without warrant upon reasonable suspicion that someone is committing an offence (s.4(3)). Where the offence has ceased then the provisions of s.25 Police and Criminal Evidence Act 1984 will apply. A suitable statement of reasons might be "threatening behaviour" or "provoking violence" or "causing fear of violence". For a power of entry to arrest, see s.17(1)(c) Police and Criminal Evidence Act 1984, as amended by Sch.2 para.7.

(i) Trial

The offence is triable summarily only (s.4(4)).

(j) Duplicity

In order to avoid suggestions of duplicity, s.7(2) provides that s.4 creates one offence only. This was the position under s.5 of the 1936 Act; see *Vernon* v *Paddon*. See also, for the amendment of an information on appeal, *Garfield* v *Maddocks* where an amendment from threatening to insulting behaviour was not allowed since it changed the basis on which the prosecution had been launched.

5.3 Offensive conduct (s.5)

(a) Introduction

Section 5 is a most important and innovative section, which has prompted much debate and concern. One criticism is its lack of certainty. This was recognised by the government in its White Paper:

> "It is not easy to define the offence in a manner which conforms with the normally precise definitions of the criminal law, but which at the same time is sufficiently general to catch the variety of the conduct aimed at."

The apparent generality of the offence was tempered at one stage by the requirement that someone should actually have been harassed, alarmed or distressed to a substantial degree. This dual requirement was not incorporated into the Act. It has been suggested that s.5 represents a lowering of the threshold of criminal activity and that it will be difficult to police. Indeed, the scope of s.5 is very wide and it may be applied to conduct which could on the one hand have been charged under s.4 or which on the other hand would not previously have been unlawful (nor have amounted to a breach of the peace). The government intended to provide an offence suitable to encompass minor acts of hooliganism not otherwise falling within the scope of s.4 of the Act. The White Paper describes the mischief:

"3.22 ..... Instances of such behaviour might include: hooligans on housing estates causing disturbances in the common parts of blocks of flats, blockading entrances, throwing things down the stairs, banging on doors, peering in at windows, and knocking over dustbins; groups of youths persistently shouting abuse and obscenities or pestering people waiting to catch public transport or to enter a hall or cinema; someone turning out the light in a crowded dance hall, in a way likely to cause panic; rowdy behaviour in the streets late at night which alarms local residents. .....

3.24 ..... The police have sometimes been reluctant to use section 5 of the 1936 Act to deal with minor acts of hooliganism. They do not wish to over-react to such incidents by charging too serious an offence with a disproportionately high maximum penalty; and the courts have on occasion deprecated the use of section 5 in cases where it was doubtful whether the conduct in question amounted to 'threatening, abusive or insulting words or behaviour'. These reasons would apply also to section [4 of the 1986 Act].

3.25 Even if it amounts to threatening, abusive or insulting behaviour, disorderly conduct of this sort may not be caught by section [4] ..... because it may not be likely to cause fear of violence to people or property. This may be because the fear engendered is not directed to any specific result likely to follow from the conduct but instead consists of a more general state of anxiety or alarm."

(b) The elements of the new offence

Section 5(1) provides:

"A person is guilty of an offence if he -
(a) uses threatening, abusive or insulting words or behaviour, or disorderly behaviour, or
(b) displays any writing, sign or other visible representation which is threatening, abusive or insulting,
within the hearing or sight of a person likely to be caused harassment, alarm or distress thereby."

Although there are clear similarities between s.4 and s.5 (eg the criteria of threatening, abusive or insulting, the venue), there are important distinctions:

- the criteria in s.5 are extended by the addition of "disorderly" to the list of prohibited behaviour (but not words);
- fear or provocation of violence in s.4 is replaced by likelihood of harassment, alarm or distress in s.5;
- the words "towards another person" in s.4 are omitted from s.5;
- s.5 extends only to the display and not distribution of writing, signs etc. Thus it does not extend to letters, eg poison pen letters, or the posting of leaflets through a door.

(c) Mens rea

This is the same as for s.4. There must exist an intention that (or recklessness whether) the conduct should have the necessary character (s.6(4)).

(d) The venue

Section 5 penalises conduct which occurs in private or public places subject to a restriction in the case of dwellings (s.5(2)), and see also the defence in s.5(3)(b) (page (98).

There seems to be no reason why the offence should not be applied to domestic disputes of all descriptions (provided not all participants are within a dwelling).

(e) The nature of the conduct

There must be either the use of threatening, abusive or insulting words (s.5(1)(a)) or threatening, abusive or insulting or disorderly behaviour (s.5(1)(a)) or the display of any writing, sign or visible representation which is threatening abusive or insulting (s.5(1)(b)). For the sake of conciseness the conduct as a whole will be referred to as "offensive behaviour", a description which is not used in s.5 except in the context of arrest for the offence (s.5(4)). Display only is prohibited, not distribution. The distribution of literature might be dealt with under s.4. It might also be argued that the distribution of offensive literature might amount to disorderly conduct.

For the meaning of "threatening, abusive or insulting", see page 80.

(f) "Disorderly"

"Disorderly" has been used to describe different types of conduct and has been described as:

> " ..... rather a weazel word; it might mean disorderly in the sense of riotous or the sort of conduct which is inferred in the well-known phrase 'disorderly house'; or it might mean ..... any conduct which is contrary to orders'" (*Martin* v *Yorkshire Imperial Metals Ltd*).

It is best known in the offence of "drunk and disorderly" (s.91 Criminal Justice Act 1967) which is of ancient origin. Much of the conduct which falls within s.91 may also fall within s.5. But it is possible that s.5 will come under close judicial scrutiny so that more precise guidance may be given to the meaning of the word. It may also be the case that the context will demand a different approach.

The meaning of disorderly will be derived from its context, ie its relationship to the remainder of the list (threatening, abusive and insulting), and the impact upon people who witness it, ie there must be conduct which is conducive to creating extreme concern in victims. It is an ordinary English word and needs no definition, see *Brutus* v *Cozens*. Regard must be had to the circumstances in which the conduct occurs in order to determine whether or not it merits the appellation "disorderly". The conduct of a football crowd would be disorderly if it were to be repeated in a theatre during a performance. Whilst the list of words in ss.4 and 5 are often taken to represent a descending order of seriousness, they are really no more than different types of conduct which are penalised because of their likely or intended impact upon others, ie the threat of violence or harassment etc.

Some guidance as to the meaning of "disorderly" may be obtained from New Zealand case law, where it was used in s.3.D Police Offences Amendment Act No 2 1960 (see now s.4(1)(a) Summary Offences Act 1981):

"Every person commits an offence ..... who ..... behaves in a riotous, offensive, threatening, insulting or disorderly manner .....".

The leading authority on disorderly conduct is the New Zealand Court of Appeal case of *Melser & Others* v *Police*. The following useful comments were made and because of the context of the offence these may go some way to forecast the possible view of the English courts. The additional factor in s.5 is that there must be likelihood of harassment, alarm or distress:

" ..... not only must the behaviour seriously offend against those values of orderly conduct which are recognised by right-thinking members of the public but it must at least be of a character which is likely to cause annoyance to others who are present ......"

"..... the collation of the words show that they are directed to conduct which at least is likely to cause a disturbance or annoyance to others. To lay down a wider test would, I think, be contrary to the public interest and might unduly restrict the actions of citizens who, for one reason or another, do not accept the values of orderly conduct which at the time are recognised by other members of the public. In short, there must be reasonable room for change in habits and behaviour." (*per* North P).

"Disorderly conduct is conduct which is disorderly: it is conduct which, while sufficiently ill-mannered, or in bad taste, to meet with the disapproval of well-conducted and reasonable men and women, is also something more - it must, in my opinion, tend to annoy or insult such persons as are faced with it - and sufficiently deeply or seriously to warrant the interference of the criminal law.

Just as ..... it is not enough that the conduct charged should be disapproved by the majority as merely ill-mannered or in bad taste, it is also apparent, ... that it cannot on the other hand be necessary to go so far as to prove a likely or imminent breach of the peace." (*per* Turner J)

In New Zealand, conduct falling within "disorderly" has included: a man persistently following a young woman at night thereby causing her distress (*Police* v *Christie*); demonstrators chaining themselves to the front door of the Parliament building to protest about the Vietnam war during a visit by the US Vice President (*Melser & Others* v *Police*); carrying and displaying a wreath on Anzac Day where the wreath carried a visible message protesting about the Vietnam war (*Wainwright* v *Police*); throwing a can at a crowded cricket match (*Wilde* v *Police*); invading the pitch during an international rugby match to protest about apartheid; nude bathing at a beach (*Rogers* v *Police*); disturbing court proceedings. Paddling in a duck pond in an ornamental public garden after a pop concert was not disorderly conduct (*Kinney* v *Police*: "the ducks seemed unperturbed ..... the attitude of the goldfish [was] unknown.")

Disorderly behaviour has been considered in Scotland. In

Campbell v *Adair* a bus inspector investigated a complaint that a woman had boarded a bus improperly. He upbraided the woman and interviewed her in a bullying fashion despite the fact that she was badly shaken after a fall from the bus. The inspector was found guilty of disorderly behaviour under the Glasgow Police Act 1866 (riotous, disorderly or indecent behaviour).

Conduct which may fall within s.5 can be seen in many cases. For example in *Ewart* v *Rogers* a group of youths disturbed a householder by banging on the front windows and door and smashing milk bottles. In *R* v *Newham JJ ex parte Sadiku*, urinating in public might have been classed as disorderly. Might the homosexual embracing in *Masterson* v *Holden* have been described as disorderly? Even if it could, it would have to be shown that it was within the sight or hearing of a person who was likely to be caused alarm, harassment or distress. Another common example would be a group of youths gathered in or about a shopping precinct and indulging in activities which adversely affect passers-by. In *R* v *Venna* the conduct of youths in shouting and singing and dancing in the street and banging dustbin lids was described by the court as unruly and disgraceful and anti-social. It might equally have been described as disorderly.

Whether the offence can be used to deal with noisy parties is not clear. If the only people likely to suffer harassment, alarm or distress are people within their houses then the offence will not be made out if the party itself is in a dwelling-house; but otherwise if it is in another place. Equally it may be difficult to class such parties as disorderly. This was the view of the government during debate in the House of Commons. However, since the totality of the conduct is to be taken into account such parties might constitute disorderly conduct in those cases where individuals have suffered on more than one occasion and are "at the end of their tether."

(g) Within hearing or sight

The conduct must occur within the hearing or sight of a person likely to be caused harassment, alarm or distress. There is no requirement that a victim should give evidence or that someone need be shown to have been harassed, alarmed or distressed. It must be shown that the conduct did in fact occur within the sight or hearing of a person and that the person was likely to be caused harassment, alarm or distress by such conduct. The offence is based upon likely consequences, not intended or actual consequences. Should there be witnesses who can relate their feelings then the task of the prosecution will be that much easier. Even if such witnesses cannot be found, or are unwilling to give evidence, the prosecution may still succeed, although the difficulties inherent in this are apparent. The absence of a requirement to produce a victim who was actually harassed, alarmed or distressed was a deliberate step by the government to avoid cases where a victim would be too nervous or frail to give evidence. The Minister of State at the Home Office observed that:

"The prosecution will not necessarily have to produce the victim in court, but it will have to identify in each case who it was who was likely to be alarmed ..... The court's mind will be concentrated upon the impact or likely impact of the defendant's behaviour on those who were around at that time." (HC Deb Vol 96 No 104 Col 964).

That the offensive conduct was within the sight or hearing of such a person is an inference which may drawn from the facts as a whole, eg offensive conduct in a shopping precinct where it is likely that a police officer will be able to relate only that there were shoppers who hurried away apparently upset or annoyed. Where there is noise late at night in the vicinity of an old peoples' home then the burden of showing that a person is likely to be harassed, alarmed or distressed may be relatively simple to discharge.

The defendant would appear to have to take his victims as he finds them and if they are especially timid and easily harassed etc, then, upon proof of this fact (which may involve them having to give evidence, for example where a person would not normally be adversely affected), the defendant can properly be convicted. He may be able, however, to maintain a defence under s.5(3)(a).

(h) Harassment; alarm; distress

"Harassment", "alarm" and "distress" are not defined. Since they are ordinary words of the English language and are not intended to have any special meaning they should be given their ordinary meaning; see *Brutus* v *Cozens*. They are strong words and should not be equated with "annoyance" or "disturbance" or "aggravation"; they indicate a level of extreme concern. It is worthwhile reiterating that just as a police officer may fear the use of unlawful violence so too may he be likely to be harassed, alarmed or distressed. But the level of tolerance which may be expected of a police officer may be rather higher than that of the ordinary citizen.

(i) Specific defences to s.5 offences

There are three defences specified in s.5(3) which must be established by the defendant on the balance of probabilities. The defences apply to all offences under s.5:

- *That the defendant has no reason to believe that there was any person within sight or hearing who was likely to be caused harassment, alarm or distress* (s.5(3)(a)).

This defence is likely to be of widespread utility. Not only must the absence of belief be genuine but the defendant must also, objectively, have had no reasonable grounds for the belief. Of the need to provide this sort of defence Mr Giles Shaw, Minister of State remarked in the committee stage of the Bill:

"We wanted to provide a defence for the defendant who was not aware and has no reason to be aware that his behaviour is likely to cause alarm, harassment or distress, and we wanted to bring within the offence people whose behaviour would be unlikely to harass a normal victim but who used their knowledge of the victim's weakness to make life miserable for a vulnerable person." (House of Commons Standing Committee G Col 236).

In *Masterson* v *Holden* the activity occurred in the presence of people who were distressed and roused to anger. It would be a defence to s.5 to demonstrate that the couple had no reason to believe that there was anyone in the vicinity who was likely to be harassed etc, eg because of the cosmopolitan nature of the district. This illustrates an important difference between s.4 and s.5. In s.4 conduct must be used towards another person and this suggests knowledge or recklessness on the defendant's part. In s.5 these words are not used and the conduct need not be aimed at anyone; absence of reasonable belief as to the presence of the affected person will provide a defence.

It will also be remembered that the prosecution must establish an intention to use offensive behaviour; the proximity of other people may be relevant also to that point.

• *That he was inside a dwelling and had no reason to believe that the offensive conduct would be heard or seen by a person outside that or any other house* (s.5(3)(b)).

This defence is likely to be of limited application since the offence will rarely be committed when the defendant is inside a dwelling (s.5(2)).

• *That his conduct was reasonable* (s.5(3)(c)).

The circumstances will dictate when conduct can be said in the first place to be offensive and if it can be said to be offensive then it is at the same time difficult to see how it can be reasonable. The scope of this particular defence is uncertain, not the least because, for the prosecution to succeed, it will have to establish an intention to use offensive conduct (s.5(4)). Little guidance was given during the passage of the Bill as to the likely scope of this defence. In Committee it was said that the defence was intended as "a general safety net". There was a suggestion that some high jinks might "induce a modest level of offence" and that it would be wrong to use the offence for that type of activity. Unfortunately no examples were given which might explain these ambiguous observations. In *Kinney* v *Police*, the court felt that the New Zealand offence ought not to be allowed to "scoop up all sorts of minor trouble". It was not designed to "enable the police to discipline every irregular or inconvenient or exhibitionist activity or to put a criminal sanction on over-exuberant behaviour". In addition, in Committee, it was suggested that there were examples of behaviour which might be reasonable on the basis that they came close to lawful authority, eg "if firemen or police officers use strong language when they want people to get out of the way, that may be deemed unreasonable to some but in the context would probably be acceptable." The practical nature of the examples may be doubted, cf *Campbell* v *Adair*. More to the point might be cases where offensive behaviour is used by an occupier in an attempt to rid himself of trespassers; will the use of offensive conduct be "reasonable"? Would it make any difference if the trespassers were police officers (compare the behaviour in *Marsh* v *Arscott*)? To what extent will the abuse which is commonly hurled at those who cross picket lines be reasonable, eg the shouts of "scab" or "blackleg"?

(j) Arrest and trial

It seems probable that whether s.4 or s.5 is charged will, to a large extent, depend upon prosecution policy within differing police force areas. The well known and rehearsed strictures of the courts in the use of s.5 of the 1936 Act (see *R* v *Venna*; *Ward* v *Holman*; *Wilson* v *Skeock*; *Parkin* v *Norman*) are no longer fully applicable. It is quite clear that (like the 1936 Act) the Act is aimed at more than para-military style groups and disturbances at political meetings. However, the comments of the court in *Parkin* v *Norman* are worthy of recall:

"Where the words of a statutory provision aptly describe the conduct complained of there can be no objection in law to framing a charge under that provision. But these cases demonstrate the difficulties which can sometimes occur when behaviour is charged under a provision which was never designed to deal with it."

Section 4 is specifically designed to deal with activities which are likely to lead to fear of or provocation to violence. Section 5 is specifically designed to deal with activities which lead to a serious degree of discomfort. This is not to say that, in appropriate instances, conduct which falls squarely within s.4 may not be dealt with under s.5.

A constable, in uniform or not, may arrest without warrant in the circumstances set out in s.5(4) and (5).

The first reference in s.5(4) to "he engages" must be read as meaning "is engaged in" and not "is or has been engaged in". By the nature of the offence it will be unusual for a constable to be able to witness the actual conduct and to issue a warning whilst it is continuing. If this interpretation is correct then the power of arrest will be exercised on few occasions. However, the power of arrest under s.25 Police and Criminal Evidence Act 1984 will, of course, be available if any of the general arrest conditions in that Act are satisfied.

The meaning of "shortly" or "immediately" is a question of fact for each case. "Immediately" would appear to be superfluous since any activity which occurs immediately can be said to have occurred shortly.

For duplicity, see s.7.

For sentence, see s.5(6).

(k) Other relevant offences

There are several Acts which have survived despite containing provisions which might conveniently have been encompassed within the terms of the Act. Some of these are relatively unknown, eg disorderly behaviour under the Library Offences Act 1898. More commonly known Acts include:

Section 1 Public Meeting Act 1908: It is an offence to act or incite others to act in a disorderly manner for the purpose of preventing the transaction of business of a lawful public meeting. It is also an offence to fail to give one's name and address to a constable when properly requested (s.1(3)). The meeting must be shown to be lawful; a meeting on the highway is not for these purposes necessarily unlawful (*Burden v Rigler*). The provisions as to arrest for failure to give name and address to a police officer acting on behalf of the chairman were repealed by s.7 Police and Criminal Evidence Act 1984, s.25 of which now contains the effective power to arrest in these situations. Insofar as meetings of local authorities are concerned, reference may also be made to the Public Bodies (Admissions to Meetings) Act 1960 (see now also Local Government Access to Information Act 1985 s.1 which creates s.100A of the Local Government Act 1972). Generally the public are allowed access to meetings of local authorities, but for the preservation of order there is a saving in respect of powers to suppress or prevent disorderly conduct or other misbehaviour at a meeting. This preserves the common law power to expel or exclude from a meeting those who are causing or threatening disruptive behaviour. It is also possible to exercise the power in advance of the meeting provided that the discretion to do so is exercised properly; see *R v Brent Health Authority, ex parte Francis*.

Section 97 Representation of the People Act 1983 makes it an offence to act or incite another to act in a disorderly manner with the purpose of preventing the transaction of business at certain election meetings specified in the Act. The arrest provisions, which were similar to those in the Public Meetings Act 1908, have been repealed by Sch.7 Police and Criminal Evidence Act 1984, and s.25 of that Act represents the effective arrest power.

Both s.97 and s.1 of the 1908 Act are rarely invoked. The common law power to control those threatening to break or actually breaking the peace allows ample scope to police officers and stewards, although the common law power is not confined to public meetings and may be invoked by any owner (or other person), eg a theatre or cinema manager. Putting questions to a speaker, shouting "hear hear" or simple disapproval are insufficient to merit action under the Acts; see *Wooding* v *Oxley.*

Section 2 Ecclesiastical Courts Jurisdiction Act 1860 is unaffected by the Act. Though an old Act it is not obsolete. It has its origins in the common law and several earlier statutes. It was reviewed by the Law Commission in its report on *Offences against Public Worship* (No 145), which favoured its retention. The Act penalises "riotous, violent or indecent behaviour" at any time in churchyards, burial grounds, churches, chapels or any other certified place of religious worship. There is also an offence of molesting, letting, disturbing, vexing or troubling preachers or ministers during the course of a service. Offenders are liable on summary conviction to punishment by a fine on Level 1 or two months imprisonment without fine. For cases see *R* v *Farrant* - using magic incantations at night in a churchyard; *Abrahams* v *Cavey* - interrupting a methodist service to protest about Vietnam was indecent behaviour. Interrupting a church service to complain about the church's views on Sunday trading was held to fall within the Act and merit a £30 fine (see The Times 22 May 1986). There are certain other minor Acts which relate to disturbances in cemeteries and burial grounds which were recommended for repeal by the Law Commission but which are still extant.

5.4 Racial hatred (Part III)

(a) Background

At common law little protection was given to racial groups in respect of incitement to hatred. Sedition was possibly committed by such incitement. Section 5 of the 1936 Act could have been used in appropriate circumstances although reliance on breach of the peace restricted its usefulness and it was ineffective against more insidious forms of incitement, or incitements which occurred privately. Section 6 Race Relations Act 1965 was the first statutory provision to attempt specifically to deal with the mischief but that too suffered from certain restrictive provisions, eg the need to prove both an intention to incite racial hatred and a likelihood of racial hatred being stirred up. Section 70 Race Relations Act 1976 introduced s.5A into the 1936 Act. This was substantially the same as s.6 Race Relations Act, although the need to prove intent was removed and the likelihood of racial hatred being stirred up became the sole test. The section, however, maintained restrictive measures, eg it did not contain a power of arrest; there was a limited scope to publication and distribution which did not deal with distribution of material to members of a club or organisation. There were also provisions in other Acts dealing with incitements to racial hatred, eg Cable and Broadcasting Act 1984 and the Theatres Act 1968; these together with s.5A have now been largely repealed (Sch.3) and six new offences have been created in ss.18-23.

(b) Racial hatred (s.17)

The hatred to be stirred up must be against a group in Great Britain. The definition of "group" in s.17 has been adapted from the Race Relations Act 1976. The definition is wide enough to cover Jews (*Seide* v *Gillette*) and Sikhs (*Mandla* v *Dowell Lee*), as well as many other groups. The meaning of "ethnic origins" was considered in *Mandla* v *Dowell Lee*, where the House of Lords provided guidelines as to the criteria for deciding whether a group can be classed as having ethnic origins.

(c) Words, behaviour and display of written material (s.18)

It is an offence (a) to use threatening, abusive or insulting words or behaviour; or (b) to display threatening, abusive or insulting written material, either where the defendant intends racial hatred to be stirred up by such use, or where, having regard to all the circumstances, racial hatred is likely to be stirred up by such use. "Gestures" are not expressly within the section although they will be included in behaviour, thus in appropriate circumstances a nazi style salute would fall within the section, as might a clenched fist salute. Certain words or behaviour are not included; see s.18(6) and s.22(1). "Written material" is defined in s.29. "Display" is not restricted to display to the public or a section of it.

(d) Venue

The Act prohibits conduct generally in public and private places. Even where the offending words or behaviour are used in a private place, eg at a private meeting, an offence may still be made out. The only restriction is that there is no offence where the prohibited conduct occurs in a dwelling (which is defined in s.29) and is observed only by people inside that or any other house. If it is observed outside a dwelling-house then there will still be a defence for the defendant who is able to show on the balance of probabilities that he was inside a dwelling-house and had no reason to believe that the conduct would be observed by a person outside that house and not in another dwelling (s.18(4)). Where the conduct occurs in any other place, eg at a factory, club or private meeting the defence will not apply.

(e) "Threatening"; "abusive"; "insulting"

These words will be interpreted as for s.4 and s.5; see page 80. The difficulty identified by commentators is that whilst blatant propaganda can be brought within the scope of the Act, more sophisticated propaganda may not. Such propaganda may sufficiently obfuscate the issues so as to ensure that the "ordinary person" could not perceive them as falling within the appropriate categories, eg if the matter purports to have an "educational" flavour. Brownlie observes that the formula is not very helpful and "at least superfluous" and "likely to have a restrictive effect". Where spoken words or behaviour are used a prosecution under s.18 may be sustained but before a mixed audience (ie not composed of like-minded people), offences contrary to s.4 or s.5 may be easier to establish.

Where a person is not shown to have intended to stir up racial hatred (ie where the prosecution is able to prove likelihood) it will be necessary for the prosecution to establish that a person did intend his words or behaviour to be threatening, abusive or insulting, or was reckless as to that (s.18(5)).

(f) Intention or likelihood

All the offences now adopt the alternative of either intent to stir up racial hatred or the likelihood of racial hatred being stirred up. This is a shift from s.5A of the 1936 Act which relied on likelihood alone. Section 5A was defective since it did not deal with those occasions on which inflammatory words or material might be addressed to the like minded observer, who would be encouraged further, or to those who are unsympathetic but unlikely to be affected in such a way. The nature of the material may well indicate unequivocally the intention of the defendant. If this cannot be shown it will be necessary to demonstrate the likelihood of racial hatred being stirred up. The words "in all the circumstances" indicate that regard should be had to the facts surrounding each event. Words or gestures which are threatening, abusive or insulting and which might be likely to stir up racial hatred in some circumstances might not be likely to do so in other circumstances. There is the world of difference between threatening, abusive or insulting material displayed during a respectable seminar discussing problems of racial harassment and such display at a meeting to promote the views of a particular organisation.

(g) Arrest

A constable, in uniform or not, may arrest without warrant a person he reasonably suspects is committing an offence (s.18(3)). Where this is not applicable, eg because the conduct has stopped, then recourse may be had to s.25 Police and Criminal Evidence Act 1984.

(h) Publication and distribution of racially inflammatory written material (s.19)

It is an offence to publish or distribute threatening, abusive or insulting written material either with intent to stir up racial hatred or whereby it is likely that racial hatred will be stirred up (s.19(1)(a), (b)). For the meaning of "threatening" etc, see page 80. Where a person is not shown to have intended to stir up racial hatred (ie where the prosecution is able to prove likelihood) it will be a defence for the defendant to prove that he was not aware of the content of the material and did not suspect or have reason to suspect that it was threatening etc (s.19(2)). For the meaning of "written material" see s.29. For the meaning of "writing" see Interpretation Act 1978 Sch.1. It includes typing, printing and photography, but does not extend to videos or films (but see in this respect ss.21 and 22).

The application of "publishes" and "distributes" are restricted by s.19(3) to publication or distribution to the public or a section of the public, and the meaning of publish or distribute is not otherwise defined.

Publication or distribution to the members of an association to which the defendant belonged was not an offence under the amended 1936 Act. This restriction has been removed. Thus the private circulation of material within an association will be an offence provided (a) it can be said to be publication or distribution to "the public or a section of the public" and (b) there is the necessary intention or likelihood.

The meaning of "section of the public" is not entirely certain. Whilst it is clear that the intention of Parliament was to include members of associations generally within the definition, it is not clear whether members of a "club" will also be within the scope of the Act. Although it dealt with an earlier Act, *Charter* v *Race Relations Board* appears to be persuasive of the point that a genuine club exercising strict membership restrictions would not be a section of the public for the purposes of the Act. However, since that case concerned the supply of goods or services such result need not flow inexorably for the purposes of the offences under the Act.

For an example of the judicial approach to the meaning of publication or distribution see *R* v *Britton* where the court took a pragmatic view of publication and distribution. Leaving pamphlets in the front porch of an MP's house was capable of being a distribution. Had the pamphlets been visible from the road there might also have been a publication. However, in that case the distribution had not been to a "section of the public". Posting a bill on a wall or daubing a slogan might be said to be both publication and display for the purposes of s.4.

(i) Arrest

There is no power of arrest attached to s.19. The power of arrest under s.25 Police and Criminal Evidence Act 1984 is available in appropriate circumstances.

(j) Possession of racially inflammatory written material or recordings (s.23).

A person commits an offence if:

(i)   he has in his possession threatening, abusive or insulting written material or a recording of such visual images or sounds,

(ii) with a view to the purposes specified in s.23(1)(a) and (b), provided

(iii) he intends racial hatred to be stirred up or it is likely to be stirred up.

"Written material" and other terms in s.23 are explained in s.29. Section 23 does not extend to possession for certain purposes outlined in s.23(4). The purposes in s.23(1)(a) and (b) include publication, distribution, showing or playing, and these must be to the public or a section of the public (see ss.29, 19(3) and 21(2)). "Display" is also included but does not appear to be so restricted, although it must presumably be a display for the purposes of s.18. For the meaning of "section of the public" see the comments above.

Possession of a video recording or film is within s.23. It is thus complementary to s.21 which prohibits the distribution, showing or playing of, *inter alia*, video recordings. A person who receives a video recording or film for editing purposes or as part of a chain of distribution will be in possession of the recording even though the actual distribution etc may be by another person. Insofar as written material is concerned s.23 is complementary to ss.18 (display) and 19 (distribution or publication). The cases on other areas of law (eg unlawful possession of drugs or firearms) will be of assistance in determining both the physical element of possession and the required mental element. The offence is not "knowingly possess"; the defendant need only know that he has some written matter or recording. Accordingly, there is a defence of innocent possession in s.23(3) which may be of assistance to anyone who is not shown to have intended to stir up racial hatred. This may apply to a firm which delivers a bundle of leaflets to an address of a political party (provided this can be said to be possession within the Act).

The defence must prove the relevant matters upon the balance of probabilities.

A journalist who has collected racially inflammatory material for research purposes will not commit an offence under s.23 if he intends only to use it as background material. If he intends that it should be published in whole or in part then, if he has an intention that racial hatred should be stirred up, he may be convicted. If this is not his intention, regard should be had to the circumstances of the proposed publication etc in deciding whether or not racial hatred is likely to be stirred up, eg publication in a respectable social science journal or as part of a genuine educational programme (s.23(2)). There is no power of arrest attached to s.23. The power of arrest under s.25 Police and Criminal Evidence Act 1984 is available in appropriate circumstances.

There is power for a justice of the peace to issue a search warrant to search for material falling within s.24 (1), (3) and (4). For procedures in connection with search warrants and their execution see Police and Criminal Evidence Act 1984.

(k) Plays, recordings, broadcasts and cable programmes

It is an offence to present or direct a public performance of a play which involves the use of threatening, abusive or insulting words or behaviour with the intention thereby to stir up racial hatred or whereby, in all the circumstances, racial hatred is likely to be stirred up (s.20). These provisions replace those in the Theatres Act 1968 which dealt with incitement to racial hatred.

It is an offence for a person to distribute, show or play a recording of visual images or sounds which are threatening, abusive or insulting if he intends thereby to stir up racial hatred or whereby racial hatred is likely to be stirred up (s.21). This offence is intended to deal with the use of video or other recordings which are used to promote racially inflammatory propaganda. There is evidence of the growth of video recordings for this purpose. The offence is not restricted to particular venues and may be committed in both public and private places, eg private meetings in a dwelling-house. The distribution etc must be to the public or a section of the public (s.21(2)) and in some instances there may be doubt as to what is a section of the public for this purpose; eg see *Charter* v *Race Relations Board.*

Certain persons identified in s.22(2) may be guilty of an offence if a programme involving threatening, abusive or insulting visual images or sounds is broadcast or is included in a cable programme service. There must be either intent or likelihood of racial hatred being stirred up. The offences do not extend to certain broadcasts or cable programmes (s.22(7)). Section 29 explains the terms used in s.23. Certain minor changes are made to the Cable and Broadcasting Act 1984; the amendments are clearly set out in Sch.2 para.5.

There are no powers of arrest attached to any of these offences; the provisions of s.25 Police and Criminal Evidence Act 1984 apply.

(l) Miscellaneous matters which apply to Part III

Section 26 protects certain reports of court and Parliamentary proceedings.

A court must order forfeiture upon conviction where it convicts for an offence contrary to either s.18 and the offence relates to written material or ss.19, 21 or 23 (s.25). The court must order forfeiture of all written materials or recordings produced to it and shown to be materials or recordings to which those offences apply.

Bodies corporate: where offences are committed by bodies corporate s.28 provides that certain other people, eg directors, may also be prosecuted if it can be shown that they connived at or consented to the offence.

The consent of the Attorney General is required to all prosecutions or he must himself bring the action (s.27(1)); see page 65.

The offences are triable summarily or on indictment (s.27(3)) and are punishable by 2 years imprisonment or a fine or both upon conviction on indictment; or to imprisonment for 6 months or a fine or both upon summary conviction.

Duplicity: each of ss.18-23 creates one offence (s.27(2)).

Chapter 6

Processions and assemblies

6.1 The background

The government in its White Paper refers to a "right of peaceful protest" and a "right to march". These so-called rights are heavily circumscribed by a variety of measures, eg s.137 Highways Act 1980, bye-laws and the Act itself. The generally accepted view of rights of protest in relation to the highway is that no person has a right to use a highway for a public meeting and that a person can only use the highway for the purpose for which it has been dedicated, ie to pass and repass, and any other ancillary use. In *Duncan* v *Jones* Lord Hewitt remarked that "English law does not recognise any special right of public meeting for political or other purposes. The right of assembly ..... is nothing more than a view taken by the court of the individual liberty of the subject." However, the rights are protected by the European Convention on Human Rights and Fundamental Freedoms, which is not part of United Kingdom law. Article 10 of the ECHR protects freedom of assembly but in such terms that it is subject to restraints which are "necessary in a democratic society in the interests of public safety ..... the prevention of disorder .....". The government bore in mind the terms of the ECHR in drafting the Act but an individual petition based upon the terms of Article 10 is possible; see for example *CARAF* v *UK*.

The scope of the common law and other powers referred to in Chapters 1 and 2 indicate that the exercise of these "rights" was not easy. In addition s.3 of the 1936 Act provided a mechanism for imposing conditions or a prohibition order on processions. But there was no power in relation to assemblies which did not constitute processions. There was no advance notice requirement. A few local Acts with additional powers to control marches survived the Local Government Act 1972 but have been largely repealed by the Act; see page 22. However, the provisions requiring Codes of Practice have been retained in Greater Manchester, Cheshire, Isle of Wight and the West Midlands. Section 3 of the 1936 Act has been repealed and replaced by provisions in ss.11-16.

6.2 Election meetings

Nothing in ss.11-16 creates any rights to hold a meeting. The right to hold certain election meetings is specifically provided for in ss.95 and 96 Representation of the People Act 1983 (as slightly amended by the 1985 Representation of the People Act). Candidates in Parliamentary and local elections may use certain local authority rooms for the purposes of holding public meetings in connection with their candidacy. These rights are enforceable by private law remedies; see *Webster* v *Southwark Borough Council*; *Ettridge* v *Morrell*. A local authority may not impose a ban on a particular group (or on all groups) based on irrelevant considerations such as political views, or even for reasons which might be considered relevant, eg the risk of disorder. A refusal to allow the use of property based on an apprehension that the meeting would not be a public meeting would be permissible. For disturbances at public and election meetings see Chapter 5.

As regards other meetings on local authority property, a general ban on certain groups using public premises which are the subject of statutory regulation may be permissible and not *ultra vires* provided the discretion has been exercised properly. It will be reasonable to take into account the risk of disorder and the risk of damage to community relations (*Wheeler* v *Leicester City Council*). In other cases where there is no statutory regulation then a general ban on any grounds may be lawful. Most premises will be let under contracts which contain a clause which will allow cancellation if there is a risk of disorder or if the identity of the other contracting party has been misrepresented; see *Webster* v *Newham Borough Council; Verrall* v *Great Yarmouth Borough Council.*

6.3 Other offences or powers

The offences and powers discussed in this Chapter must always be read in conjunction with the common law powers considered in Chapter 2 and other powers contained in a variety of statutes which may be employed to control assemblies and processions. The following matters may be noted in addition to the matters discussed in earlier Chapters:

• Under s.52 Metropolitan Police Act 1839 and s.22 City of London Police Act 1839, the Commissioner of Police may make regulations and give directions to prevent the obstruction of streets in the Metropolitan Police District, eg by assemblies or processions which are capable of giving rise to obstruction of the streets or to disorder or annoyance of a kind likely to lead to breaches of the peace. These regulations and directions provide a useful form of prior control over processions and assemblies and were apparently exercised in connection with the "Stop the City" demonstrations in 1983-1984. The Town Police Clauses Act s.21 is of similar effect and applies in certain areas outside the Metropolitan Police District. For cases on these provisions, which are unaffected by the Act, see *Papworth* v *Coventry* (vigil outside an embassy), and *Brownsea Haven Properties* v *Poole Corporation.* These cases examine the construction and scope of ss.52 and 21 respectively. Both s.28 Town Police Clauses Act 1847 and s.54 Metropolitan Police Act 1839 create summary offences of obstruction to the footpaths or thoroughfares.

• Under section 137 Highways Act 1980, wilful obstruction of free passage along a highway without lawful excuse is an offence which is frequently used in respect of pickets, those who distribute leaflets, "sit-down demonstrators" and those who otherwise assemble on the highway. The Act does not affect the offence. There is no longer a specific power to arrest for obstruction of the highway although unlawful obstruction of the highway is one of the general arrest conditions in s.25 Police and Criminal Evidence Act 1984. In connection with processions and assemblies, the offence under s.137 will remain a useful additional power which may well bypass the provisions of the Act.

Standing in the highway proferring leaflets or holding banners may be an obstruction of the highway. But, to be an unlawful obstruction of the highway the prosecution must demonstrate:

   (i)   the fact of obstruction;
   (ii) that it was wilful (see *Arrowsmith* v *Jenkins* where "wilful" meant of one's own free will); and
   (iii) the absence of lawful excuse; this point will frequently turn upon the reasonableness of the user.

Magistrates must consider all of the elements (see *Hirst* v *Chief Constable of West Yorkshire*). There must be a "user" of the highway; thus compelling a vehicle to stop at a picket line will not normally entail any user of the highway (see *Jones* v *Bescoby*) and the issue of reasonableness will not arise. The classic description of reasonable user will be found in *Nagy* v *Weston*:

> "It depends upon all the circumstances, including the length of time the obstruction continues, the place where it occurs, the purpose for which it is done, and ..... whether it does in fact cause an actual obstruction as opposed to a potential obstruction."

See also *Hubbard* v *Pitt* for a view of the propriety of non-industrial picketing, this was emphasized by the court in *Hirst* v *Chief Constable of West Yorkshire*. It seems unlikely that the imposition of conditions upon an assembly in accordance with s.14 will provide a lawful authority, although it may be some evidence of reasonable user.

• Public nuisance: *Stephen's Digest of the Criminal Law* defines this as "an act not warranted by law or an omission to carry out a legal duty, which act or omission obstructs or causes inconvenience or damage to the public in the exercise of rights common to all." Demonstrations, pickets and other assemblies, usually occurring on or about the highway, may amount to the common law offence of public nuisance; see *R v Clark*; *R v Moule* and *R v Adler* for descriptions of the offence. Picketing will not necessarily constitute the offence (but see *Tynan v Balmer*); mass picketing will. In *Thomas v NUM*, Scott J remarked: " ..... if picketing ..... is peacefully and responsibly conducted ..... I can see no reason at all why it should be regarded *per se* as a common law nuisance ..... In my judgement, mass picketing is clearly ..... common law nuisance."

6.4 Public processions

(a) What are public processions?

Section 11 (advance notice), s.12 (imposition of conditions), and s.13 (prohibition orders) apply to a public procession. The definition of public procession does not contain a minimum number of participants, unlike the definition of public assembly. Under s.16 it is "a procession in a public place". A public place is defined in s.16 as:

"(a) any highway ..... and
(b) any place to which at the material time the public or any section of the public has access, on payment or otherwise, as of right or by virtue of express or implied permission."

This reflects the definition in s.1(1)(a) Police and Criminal Evidence Act 1984 (stop-search power).

To see what places might fall within (b) reference may be made to the case law on the 1936 Act which contained a similar but not identical definition; see eg *Cawley v Frost*; *Marsh v Arscott*. As well as the usual processions on the highway, a parade at an arena which precedes a rally (eg a boy scout or girl guide rally) will be a public procession for the purposes of the Act, as will an Easter parade around a church even if not on the highway.

The Oxford English Dictionary defines "procession" as: "The action of a body of persons going or marching along in orderly succession in a formal or ceremonial way ..... a body of persons marching in this way."

Flockhart v *Robinson*, which concerns principally the meaning of "organise", explained that "A procession is not a mere body of persons; it is a body of persons moving along a route." In *Kent* v *Metropolitan Police Commissioner* the Court of Appeal were not required to deal with the point but Lord Denning observed that:

> "A public procession is the act of a body of persons marching along in orderly succession - see the Oxford English Dictionary. All kinds of processions take place every day up and down the country - carnivals, weddings, funerals, processions to the Houses of Parliament, marches to Trafalgar Square and so forth."

In *Flockhart* v *Robinson*, the magistrates had found that a group of demonstrators had held a lawful procession in part of the City of London. This procession had broken up and the group moved into part of the City where processions were prohibited. The group was found to have been in "a loose formation not in ranks" and "in the form of a rabble and not a compact body". At some stage it became a procession; it came into being spontaneously and without prior arrangement. It had taken on the character of a procession by virtue of its adoption of an orderly formation.

Whether or not the necessary formation has been achieved will be a question of fact. A bus-load of soccer fans disgorged near to a soccer ground will presumably not be in such an orderly formation, but if they are marshalled by the police and marched from the car park to the ground then they may have taken on the character of a procession. A school teacher who organises her children into a crocodile will have organised a procession since the crocodile will, hopefully, have the necessary formation and cohesion. As will be seen advance notice will not have to be given of such a procession.

A single person marching cannot constitute a procession. Thus a single person might still march along a route despite a prohibition on processions. If he has the necessary notoriety then he may well attract supporters or counter-demonstrators, and hence the risk of violence, and police presence which the prohibition order sought to avoid. An illustration is the walk of a well-known individual through part of Manchester, this attracted a large group of supporters, counter-demonstrators and police officers who were obliged to keep the groups apart.

Can a series of vehicles constitute a procession for the purposes of the Act? Would a mass cycle rally or a parade of floats constitute a procession? The element of marching would be missing but it would have the orderly appearance and community of purpose demanded of a procession.

(b) Advance notice of public processions (s.11)

There is no advance notice requirement for assemblies. The object of s.11 is to prevent the mischief of processions of which the police are unaware and which may occasion public order or other problems. In most instances, advance notice will be given by the organisers as a matter of course. Advance notice is required only of certain public processions. Proposals to hold a public procession must be notified to the police if it is a procession intended to:

(i)   demonstrate support for or opposition to the views or actions of any person or body of persons (s.11(1)(a)); or

(ii) publicise a cause or campaign (s.11(1)(b)); or

(iii) mark or commemorate an event (s.11(1)(c)).

Many processions will fall into one or more categories, eg a procession to complain about plans to make employees redundant might fall within any or all of the categories.

Excluded from the categories of processions of which notice is required are:

(a) processions commonly or customarily held in that police area;
(b) funeral processions organised by a funeral director in the normal course of his business (s.11(2)).

Whether a procession is commonly or customarily held in that police area will be matter of fact. Examples will be Remembrance Day parades, Lord Mayors' parades, May Day marches, Rag parades, Easter and other religious processions, eg by sikhs to celebrate Baisakhi. There may still be occasions where there is some doubt as to whether a march will have achieved the status of being commonly or customarily held, and advance notice should be given as a matter of good practice. Where a march is commonly held (eg to celebrate so called "Bloody Sunday") it may move from area to area and thus still require advance notice.

Advance notice is not required where "it is not reasonably practicable to give any advance notice" (s.11(1)). The correct process appears to be to ask:

(i) is this procession of a type for which advance notice has to be given? If no, no advance notice is required. If yes, then:
(ii) is it reasonably practicable to give any advance notice? If no, there is no requirement to give advance notice; if yes then:
(iii) what advance notice is it practicable to give? If more than six days then give six clear days; if less than six days then give as much as reasonably practicable.

At what stage it becomes reasonably practicable to give some notice, albeit not the 6 clear days required, will be a matter of fact. In the case of a spontaneous procession, or one organised at very short notice, or springing up without prior organisation, need notice be given? Much will turn on the meaning of "any notice". In most instances, some advance notice can be given, even if only by telephoning the local police station. Does the phrase therefore mean "any notice in the prescribed form", ie written? This view would certainly be preferable and in line with the spirit of the Act. Does "any notice" mean some notice unless it would be *de minimis*; in any case what would be *de minimis*?

Suppose, in response to an event which occurs one day, a procession is organised overnight and takes place during the course of the next morning. It would be reasonably practicable to give some notice (either in the form required or orally) and failure to give written notice in the form required will constitute an offence. In this situation it would not be enough to give oral notice. Notice under the Act must always be written (s.11(1)).

Examples of spontaneous processions or processions organised at very short notice can be found. For example, where a factory closure announcement is made and the employees stop work in order to march to the company headquarters, or where a group of parents decide, on the spur of the moment after a child is injured at an accident black spot, to march in protest. The advance notice provisions apply since the processions are to demonstrate opposition to the views of a body or person and to publicise a cause or campaign. In these examples some advance notice could have been given, eg by telephone (indeed the required period could have been given if the procession has been delayed). However, under the circumstances, it could not be said that it was reasonably practicable to give any notice, and certainly not notice in the prescribed form. Accordingly no advance notice need be given. An example of a spontaneous procession would be *Flockhart* v *Robinson*.

(c) The form of the advance notice

The advance notice must:

- be in writing (s.11(1));
- be delivered to any police station in the police force area where the procession is intended to start; or in the case of a procession which will start in Scotland and cross into England, notice should be given to a police station in the first police area in England on the proposed route (s.11(4)(a), (b));
- be delivered either by hand not less than six days before the date of the procession or by recorded postal delivery provided actual delivery takes place not less than 6 clear days before the intended date of the procession (s.11(5)). The presumption of service and delivery under s.7 Interpretation Act 1978 does not apply;
- where 6 clear days notice cannot be given, be delivered by hand and as soon as delivery is reasonably practicable (s.11(6));
- specify the intended date, start time, route and the name and address of at least one of the organisers (s.11(3)).

This information is the maximum which the police can demand under the Act. It is however evident from the Code of Practice in Appendix C that much more information may be expected so that adequate policing and traffic arrangements can be made.

(d) Offences in relation to advance notice

Only the organisers of a public procession can commit offences against s.11. The offences are:

- failure to satisfy the notice requirements (s.11(7)(a));
- non-adherence to the date, time or route specified in the notice (s.11(7)(b)).

The organiser need not actually take part in the procession. The organiser may be able to prove by way of defence and on the balance of probabilities that:

- he did not know of and did not suspect or have reason to suspect the failure in s.11(7)(a) or s.11(7)(b) (s.11(8)) (This defence may impose upon organisers a requirement for good organisational practice); or
- to prove that the failure under s.11(7)(b) arose from something beyond his control and from the agreement or direction of a police officer (s.11(9)). As to the giving of directions by police officers, see page 124.

There is no power of arrest attached to s.11 but s.25 Police and Criminal Evidence Act 1984 may be used when appropriate. The offence is triable only summarily and punishable by fine (s.11(10)).

(e) Who is an organiser?

The meaning of "organiser" is important for the offences in ss.11-14. There is no definition of "organiser". Many people may assist generally in the organising of a procession, eg by arranging banners, parking, refreshments, stewards. At what stage such a person becomes an organiser is a difficult question, and this may be particularly so when the real organisers hide behind nominees or where there is much delegation.

The only case which dealt with the issue of organisers for the purposes of s.3 of the 1936 Act was *Flockhart* v *Robinson*. This case turns on its own special facts but the approach of the majority is radically different from that of the dissentient Finnemore J. The views of the majority are unlikely to be of more general application and the case will be readily distinguishable on its facts. The remarks of Finnemore J are to be preferred since they make it clear that simply stewarding a march cannot be said necessarily to amount to organising. The majority seem to have been unduly influenced by the fact that the appellant had continued to act vis-à-vis the procession in the same way as he had done when it was not unlawful. This assumed that what the appellant had been doing previously amounted to organising the procession.

" .....'organised' is not a term of art. When a procession is organised what happens? A procession is not a mere body of persons; it is a body of persons who are moving along a route. Therefore the person who organises the route is the person who organises the procession ..... If a person indicates the route, plans the route, or points out the route by which other persons are to go, I think he is organising a procession." (*per* Goddard CJ)

"The mere fact that a person takes part in a procession would not of itself be enough. I do not think that the fact that the appellant was the leading person in the procession would by itself be enough, although it might be some evidence to be considered ..... I think organising a procession means something in the nature of arranging or planning a procession. It is not necessary for the plans to be made long in advance or perhaps in advance at all ..... The procession could be organised on the spot in the street, but ..... [T]he procession formed itself spontaneously, and I do not think anything the appellant did thereafter amounted to organising that procession." (*per* Finnemore J).

6.5 Public assemblies

Prior to the Act there were no general statutory provisions for the control of public assemblies. The Act now allows certain limited conditions to be imposed upon certain public assemblies. Common law and statutory powers to control certain assemblies remain; see, eg, *Duncan* v *Jones*, page 33, s.137 Highways Act 1980; Trafalgar Square Act 1844.

"Public assembly" means an "assembly of 20 or more persons in a public place which is wholly or partly open to the air" (s.16). The word "assembly" is not further explained. The Oxford English Dictionary says that it is "gathering together, meeting, the state of being collected or gathered. The coming together of persons or things. A gathering of persons, a number of people met together." The meaning of assembly would normally incorporate processions. However, for the purposes of the Act it is assumed that the two are distinct.

Examples of assemblies within the Act are pickets, lobbies, vigils, pop festivals, queues for buses and tickets and a group of people drinking in a pub garden. It would also include football matches, and the government anticipates that the powers in s.14 might be used in that respect, eg to control the size of the crowd. The meaning is not limited to static assemblies so that a group of circulating protestors (not amounting to a procession) might be within the ambit of the Act. It is not clear whether an assembly is to be defined by reference to the location, the organisers, the participants, the objectives, or an amalgam of all four, or other, considerations. For example, a picket outside a factory might move from place to place and its participants might change from time to time. For the purposes of the Act will it always be treated as one assembly?

"Public place" is defined in s.16 so as to bring it into line with s.1(1)(a) Police and Criminal Evidence Act 1984. Some assistance as to the meaning of "public place" may be gleaned from cases on the 1936 Act, eg *Marsh* v *Arscott*, *Cawley* v *Frost*, although the definition in s.16 is slightly different to that in the 1936 Act. It is only in relation to public assemblies that the meaning of public place is likely to be an important factual issue, eg whether the entrance to a factory is a public place.

The reference to "open to the air" is reminiscent of the definition adopted by the 1936 Act, before it was amended by the Criminal Justice Act 1972. This created a category of open space and, for example, did not include a railway platform since that was an integral part of a building (see *Cooper* v *Shield*). Partly open to the air must mean more than *de minimis*. A structure with four walls but no roof might be open to the air; similarly a building with no walls but a roof. A building cannot be said to be open to the air simply because it has large and open doors. A football stand enclosed on three sides would be within the Act, as would the remainder of the ground.

In cases on the meaning of "public place" under the 1936 Act, emphasis was laid on the nature of the place as a whole. The question was whether, given that some areas might be closed to the public, taken as a whole that place was a public place. In *Cawley* v *Frost*, Lord Widgery remarked that:

> " ..... where you have an establishment which is set up to provide for the public such as the Halifax Town Football Club or Wembley Stadium, one ought to approach it on the basis that it is a public place in its entirety ..... *Prima facie* you look at the whole of the establishment and you are not ..... deterred from doing that merely by finding that certain portions of the establishment have been denied to the public for one reason or another."

A similar approach should be adopted to the meaning of "public place" and "open to the air" under the Act.

It may also be difficult to identify the physical boundaries of "the place". Suppose that a public meeting is taking place in a marquee in the grounds of a school. Is the place to be defined by relation to the physical boundaries of the tent, or the grounds? Suppose that it is a public meeting inside the school, eg an election meeting, the building cannot be said to be "wholly or partly open to the air", but the remainder of the grounds can so be described. It was not the intention of Parliament to extend the powers to impose conditions to these situations and the preferred interpretation would be the one which restricted the "public place" to the tent or the building, rather than the grounds as a whole.

It should be emphasized that the assemblies which fall within the Act are not restricted to those which are adjacent to the highway. It should also be remembered that offences contrary to ss.4 and 5 may be committed anywhere and are not restricted to public places.

6.6 Imposing conditions on processions (s.12) and assemblies (s.14)

The power in s.3 of the 1936 Act to impose conditions on

public processions was seldom used because of the close collaboration between organisers and the police. An illustration of its use would be to avoid a particularly sensitive building. Sections 12 and 14, which replace s.3, are almost identical in purport and will be dealt with together. They allow conditions to be imposed upon public processions and public assemblies. The Act does not affect the powers of the police under their preventive duty or other criminal law powers. Nor does the Act affect the civil liabilities, rights or obligations of any person, eg to obtain an injunction.

(a) Who may impose conditions?

Conditions may be imposed either before or during a procession or assembly by the senior police officer. He is:

- in relation to a procession or assembly intended to be held, the chief officer of police (ss.12(2)(b) and 14(2)(b) (subject to delegation under s.15) and the directions must be given in writing (ss.12(3) and 14(3));
- in relation to an assembly or a procession being held (or a procession intended to be held while participants are assembling), the most senior in rank of police officers at the scene (s.12(2)(a), s.14(2)(a)); the directions need not be given in writing.

The conditions may be imposed on either the organisers or those taking part. In the light of the requirement of knowledge in the offences, it would seem appropriate for the organisers to be served with a copy of the directions when given in writing, or for them to be told personally. Appropriate steps should then be taken to inform the participants at the earliest stage of proceedings and also, if appropriate and possible, when it is anticipated that there might be a breach of the conditions. It should also be made quite clear that what is being given is a direction containing conditions made under the Act; there are no procedures for this in the Act.

(b) The criteria for imposing conditions (s.12(1) and s.14(1))

The senior police officer must have regard to:

(i) the intended or actual time or place of the procession or assembly; and
(ii) the circumstances in which it will be held; and
(iii) in the case of a procession, its route.

He may impose conditions is he reasonably believes (ie actually believes on objectively reasonable grounds):

- the procession or assembly may result in serious public disorder, serious damage to property or serious disruption to the life of the community (s.12(1)(a), s.14(1)(a)); or
- the purpose of the organisers is to intimidate others (s.12(1)(b), s.14(1)(b)).

Serious public disorder and serious damage to property

Lord Scarman in his report on the Brixton riots took the view that the word "serious" added nothing to the expression "public disorder". But, it does seem that the phrase is suitable to describe the extent of disorder, eg the disorder seen during the miners' strike, or in the Wapping dispute. Whether the degree of disorder or damage will be serious must be judged from the objective standpoint of the senior police officer, not the individuals who are likely to be affected.

Serious disruption to the life of the community

Most processions will involve some element of disruption to the life of a community, eg traffic hold-ups or difficulties in shopping or delivering goods. Serious disruption might occur when a procession or assembly would effectively deny local residents access to and from their homes or places of work or leisure pursuits. The White Paper proposal included the word "normal" to qualify "life". Its absence from the Act is not significant and does emphasize that processions are themselves part of the life of a community, albeit one in which not everyone indulges.

"Community" is not qualified. Would it be enough that disruption was to be caused to only one part of the wider community? A procession through a suburb may well cause severe disruption to that area; will that be treated as "the community"? A picket outside a furriers on a High Street may be unlikely to cause serious disruption to the town as a whole; a mass picket outside printing works may well cause serious disruption to the immediate locality. In each case what is the community which is threatened with disruption? A procession through Oxford Street will cause massive disruption but will this be tested against the community in that area or the Metropolitan District as a whole?

There is nowhere in s.12 or s.14 any mention of costs of policing processions - marches by one organisation in Lewisham and Leicester in 1980 and 1979 resulted in policing and related costs of £300,000 and £197,000 respectively. Nor is there any mention of reliance on home force manpower alone. In reality there are few forces which can cope with a major procession relying on its own manpower alone. Normally forces have to "borrow" under mutual aid agreements. Consideration of manpower and costs are not included in the Act as grounds for imposing conditions or banning orders.

Intimidation

Section 12(1)(b) and s.14(1)(b) are based upon s.7 Conspiracy and Protection of Property Act 1875 whereby it is an offence to intimidate "with a view to compel any other person to abstain from doing or to do an act which such other person has a legal right to do or abstain from doing". There has been added to s.7 of that Act a power for a constable to arrest without warrant and upon reasonable suspicion (Sch.2 para. 1).

The mischief identified by the White Paper is the organisation of a procession or assembly with "malicious intent", ie the coercion of others. The introduction of this criterion is said by the government in its White Paper to be a "libertarian safeguard designed to prevent demonstrations whose overt purpose is to persuade people from being used as a cloak by those whose real purpose is to intimidate or coerce."

Many processions and assemblies have as their object the persuasion of others, eg local councillors, government officials, MPs. Many will have implied threats, eg that the protestors will not vote in a particular fashion or will withdraw support, or even the threat of strike action. Such processions will be unlikely to amount to intimidation. "Intimidate" in the context of s.7 Conspiracy and Protection of Property Act 1875 has been judicially explained. Lord Coleridge CJ said:

"intimidate is not .....a term of art - it is a word of common speech and everyday use; and it must receive, therefore, a reasonable and sensible interpretation according to the circumstances of the cases as they arise from time to time."

Violence or threats of violence to the person fall within the meaning of intimidation and, despite initial doubts, so will threats or violence towards property. In *R* v *Jones*, it was said:

"'intimidate' in this section includes putting persons in fear by the exhibition of force or violence or the threat of force or violence; and there is no limitation restricting the meaning to cases of violence or threats of violence to the person."

It is assumed that for the purposes of the Act the word will receive a similar interpretation.

A picket in the form of a mass demonstration is likely to intimidate others and to fall within the ambit of s.14. Appropriate conditions could be imposed either on the basis of intimidation or the threat of serious public disorder.

One difficulty with s.12(1)(b) and s.14(1)(b) is that the purpose of the organisers must be established to the reasonable belief (not suspicion) of the senior police officer. In many instances the organisers will have mixed motives. Their purpose can only be inferred from the circumstances (in the absence of admissions) and in these circumstances conditions on the basis of the threat of serious disorder would be appropriate. However, where the picketing consists of mass picketing it will be most difficult for organisers to demonstrate a *bona fide* purpose especially in the light of the observations of Scott J in *Thomas* v *NUM*:

" ..... counsel for the ..... defendants submitted that mass picketing (by which I understand to be meant picketing so as by sheer weight of numbers to block the entrance to premises or to prevent the entry thereto of vehicles or people) was not *per se* tortious or criminal. In my judgement, mass picketing is clearly both common law nuisance and an offence under s.7 of the 1875 Act."

Even where the activity falls short of the picketing described above, picketing may still be intimidatory if accompanied by sufficiently serious threats or violence:

" ..... the picketing ..... is of a nature and is carried out in a manner that represents an unreasonable harassment of the working miners. A daily congregation of an average 50 - 70 men hurling abuse and in circumstances that require a police presence and require the working miners to be conveyed in vehicles do not in my view leave any real room for argument." (per Scott J).

The mischief aimed at in ss.12 and 14 is of people being deterred from going about their business and day-to-day life by threats of violence. In non-industrial cases the threats may be less obvious and more likely to be economic in nature. As such they probably do not fall within the meaning of "intimidate". For example, a picket of a company to persuade it not to invest in South Africa or not to experiment on animals might be backed up by threats of disinvestment or a campaign against the purchase or supply of that company's goods. Such action would not be intimidation. Threats of violence to the employees, directors or customers or threats against property would be intimidatory.

(c) The conditions

The conditions must be such as appear to the senior police officer to be necessary to prevent the apprehended disorder, damage, disruption or intimidation (s.12(1), s.14(1)). In other words there must be a correlation between the reason for the condition and the condition which is imposed. In the case of processions the scope of the conditions is otherwise unlimited, but in the case of assemblies the scope is limited.

• *Processions*

Any conditions may be imposed. Specifically mentioned are conditions as to the route and what might be described as "no go" areas (s.12(1)). Thus, a procession intended to pass through a racially sensitive area may properly be re-routed to avoid that area. A procession by one extreme group may be routed away from the headquarters of another group or from the route of a rival group's procession. Conditions which would normally be agreed, but which might be imposed, relate to the:

- place and time of assembly prior to the procession;
- time of departure, the route and the duration;
- carrying of flags, banners or emblems;
- use of loudhailers;
- number of persons who may march in line abreast;
- provision of stewards;
- use of vehicles in the procession.

• *Assemblies*

Conditions may relate only to the place at which the assembly may be or may continue to be held, its maximum duration and the maximum number of persons (presumably the number may not be reduced below 20). It should not be forgotten that in pursuance of their breach of the peace and other powers the real scope of police authority in this sphere is considerably wider than s.14(1) would suggest. Even though a picket may be allowed to remain on part of the highway or may be moved to another part of the highway, there may still at some future stage be an unlawful obstruction of the highway. The imposition or absence of conditions will create no immunity, although it may be some evidence of reasonable user.

Where the condition goes to the place at which an assembly may be held, a common sense view will indicate that the place may be defined negatively, ie "not within 200 yards of [a particular factory]". A common sense view will also have to be taken of when one assembly finishes and another commences. For example, if a time limit is imposed and the participants in an assembly disperse and regroup, it will be a question of fact whether or not that regrouping is a continuation of the assembly or a new assembly. Where the participants in the assembly change from time to time, as, eg, in a picket or a vigil, then a simple change in the participants would not be seen as an end of one assembly and the start of another if all the other features remain the same, eg location, objective, organisers. In any event, when the time limit expires the organisers may reduce the number of participants to below 20. It may not be sufficient to move to another place nearby.

(d) Challenge to the conditions

Since most assemblies will depend for their impact upon a particular location or time the power of the police to influence the "success" of a demonstration is clear, eg to prohibit assemblies at a particular location near the route of a ministerial visit. The use of the word "may" in s.12(1) and s.14(1) does allow challenge to the directions upon the principles of reasonableness laid down in the *Wednesbury Corporation Case*; see *Holgate-Mohammed v Duke*. Challenge may be direct by way of judicial review, or indirect as a result of prosecution under one of the offences created for breach of the conditions or under s.51 Police Act 1964.

(e) The offences

An organiser who knowingly fails to comply with a condition imposed under s.12 or s.14 will be guilty of an offence (ss.12(4) and 14(4)). The reference to a "condition imposed under this section" means a condition properly imposed. Whether a person is an organiser will be a question of fact; see *Flockhart* v *Robinson*, page 121. "Knowingly" imposes a requirement of *mens rea* and it includes deliberately closing one's mind or deliberately refraining from making enquiries. It is a defence for the organiser to prove on the balance of probabilities that "the failure arose from circumstances beyond his control" (ss.12(4) and 14(4)). The failure referred to in ss.12(4) and 14(4) is the failure of the organiser. If, despite arrangements to the contrary, a participant uses a loudhailer in breach of condition then the organiser ought not to be guilty of an offence. It would be otherwise if he authorised its use, or if he failed to give adequate information to participants. The effect of the offences may be to impose a burden upon organisers to provide adequate supervision by stewards and adequate dissemination of information about what is or is not allowed on that particular occasion. Participants who knowingly fail to comply with a condition are guilty unless they can show that the failure arose from circumstances beyond their control (ss.12(5) and 14(5)). A participant who is swept along by a crowd into a street which is not on the prescribed route may be able to show that the failure was beyond his control.

For incitement, see ss.12(6) and 14(6).

(f) Arrest

A constable in uniform may arrest without warrant anyone he reasonably suspects is committing an offence (ss.12(7) and 14(7)). For the meaning of "uniform" see *Wallwork* v *Giles*, *Taylor* v *Baldwin*. For arrest where the offence has been completed, see s.25 Police and Criminal Evidence Act 1984.

6.7 Prohibiting public processions (s.13)

(a) The procedure

A prohibition order may be imposed only on public processions; there is no power to impose a prohibition order on assemblies (but see the common law powers described in Chapter 2). Section 13 closely follows its predecessor (s.3 of the 1936 Act) and maintains the distinction in procedures between the Metropolitan Police District and City of London Police District on the one hand, and all other police force areas on the other. In the former, a prohibition order is made by the Commissioner with the consent of the Home Secretary (s.13(3), (4)). In the latter, the order is made by the District Council upon the application of the Chief Constable and with the consent of the Home Secretary (s.13(1), (2)). Neither the local authority nor the Home Secretary may institute the procedures. The prohibition order may extend to the whole or any part of the District or Metropolitan Police area as may be appropriate. The order will usually be in writing, but if not made in writing it must be reduced into writing as soon as practicable (s.13(6)).

(b) The criterion

The only criterion for imposing or requesting a prohibition order is the reasonable belief of the Chief Officer that serious public disorder cannot be prevented by the exercise of his power to impose conditions under s.12. The Chief Officer's belief will be based upon his assessment of the circumstances existing in the area and the district or part thereof, eg there may be several processions or rallies by opposing groups which would mean a large number of opponents in a small area; there may be evidence of a proposed counter demonstration or aggressive action by others; there may be factors peculiar to that district, eg a high degree of tension or a recent history of disturbances.

(c) The order

A prohibition order may be made for up to three months but

will usually be made for a much shorter period. In some instances orders for periods as short as 24 hours have been made. Periods in excess of 30 days are the exception rather than the rule. A prohibition order may be revoked or varied by a subsequent order made in the same manner as the original. The type of prohibition order favoured has been the so-called blanket ban, ie a prohibition order on all processions subject to narrowly defined exceptions; see the specimen prohibition order in Appendix B. Specific groups have not been prohibited in recent years although in 1961 the following class of procession was prohibited: "Any public procession organised by the body of persons known as the Committee of 100 or any such public procession organised by any person or persons acting on behalf of the said Committee." In 1974 one class of procession prohibited was "Any public procession in connection with the death of James McDade". Other classes on a narrower basis have included "All public processions of a political nature".

Since offences are created by s.13(7), (8) and (9), the precise nature of a prohibition order is important. Thus in 1978 a stipendiary magistrate took the view that a Trades Union traditional May Day march did not have a ceremonial nature and did not fall within that normal exception in a prohibition.

In the case of *CARAF* v *UK* the European Commission of Human Rights declared inadmissible an application which challenged, as a breach of Article 10 of the ECHR, the imposition of a blanket ban.

(d) The offences

All the offences are triable summarily; for sentence see s.13(11), (12) and (13).

Section 13(7) imposes liability upon a person who organises a procession which he knows to be prohibited (for the meaning of "organiser" see page 121). Section 13(8) imposes liability upon a person who takes part in a procession which he knows to be prohibited; s.13(9) deals with incitement to an offence under s.13(8).

(e) Arrest

A constable in uniform may arrest without warrant anyone he reasonably suspects is committing an offence under s.13 (s.13(10)). For the power to arrest where the offence has been committed or where he reasonably suspects it has been committed, see s.25 Police and Criminal Evidence Act 1984. For the meaning of "uniform" see page 132.

One particular difficulty may arise with regard to the offence under s.13(7), ie organising a public procession knowing it to be prohibited. Section 11(7) specifically provides that breach of advance notice provision is only an offence where the procession occurs; for s.13(7) this is not expressly provided. Suppose a prohibition order is in operation but nonetheless X organises a procession to take place within the period specified in the order. Can the offence be committed even though no procession in fact takes place? Could a prosecution which takes place before the date arranged for the procession succeed? The offence appears to be drawn in such terms as will allow an offence to be committed in this situation.

(f) Review of a prohibition order

Challenge to the powers exercised under s.13 may be direct by application for judicial review, or indirect by way of a defence to a prosecution for an offence under s.13, or under s.51 Police Act 1964; see *Holgate-Mohammed* v *Duke.*

In the case of *Kent* v *Metropolitan Police Commissioner* an application for judicial review was made against a decision of the Commissioner to impose a prohibition order containing the usual "blanket" prohibition. The prohibition order caught the procession proposed by CND, the Secretary General of which brought the action. It was alleged that the Commissioner had not directed his mind properly to the matters to be considered and, in particular, the fact that such a prohibition order would affect a large number of processions over a wide area. It was not alleged that CND marches had previously caused any particular problems of public disorder.

The Court of Appeal took the view that because of violence which had occurred in Brixton and at various fairs in the Metropolitan Police District, there was:

"a climate of activity ..... hooligans and others were attacking the police, who were simply doing their duty ..... they might attack the peaceful procession itself ..... This is a matter for the judgement of the Commissioner himself. When he considers the climate of activity in this city - of completely unprovoked attacks by hooligans and others - the Commissioner may well say 'There is such a risk of public disorder - even from the most peaceful demonstration being attacked by hooligans - that a ban must be imposed'."

As to the blanket nature of the prohibition order, Ackner J indicated that there was no need to use a clumsy form of drafting whch would entail reciting those classes specifically prohibited and leaving out those which should not be prohibited. Buckley P said:

"In my opinion a class or group of classes of processions can be as well identified by expressly excluding certain classes from a generality of classes as it can by listing all the classes which are not excluded."

Although the affidavit evidence of the Commissioner was described as meagre, it was not established that he had acted in bad faith or had failed to have regard to the relevant considerations.

Appendix A

Public Order Act 1986

CHAPTER 64

ARRANGEMENT OF SECTIONS

PART I

NEW OFFENCES

PART II

PROCESSIONS AND ASSEMBLIES

PART III

RACIAL HATRED

Meaning of "racial hatred"

Acts intended or likely to stir up racial hatred

A

ELIZABETH II

Public Order Act 1986

1986 CHAPTER 64

An Act to abolish the common law offences of riot, rout, unlawful assembly and affray and certain statutory offences relating to public order; to create new offences relating to public order; to control public processions and assemblies; to control the stirring up of racial hatred; to provide for the exclusion of certain offenders from sporting events; to create a new offence relating to the contamination of or interference with goods; to confer power to direct certain trespassers to leave land; to amend section 7 of the Conspiracy and Protection of Property Act 1875, section 1 of the Prevention of Crime Act 1953, Part V of the Criminal Justice (Scotland) Act 1980 and the Sporting Events (Control of Alcohol etc.) Act 1985; to repeal certain obsolete or unnecessary enactments; and for connected purposes.

[7th November 1986]

BE IT ENACTED by the Queen's most Excellent Majesty, by and with the advice and consent of the Lords Spiritual and Temporal, and Commons, in this present Parliament assembled, and by the authority of the same, as follows:—

PART I

NEW OFFENCES

1.—(1) Where 12 or more persons who are present together Riot. use or threaten unlawful violence for a common purpose and the conduct of them (taken together) is such as would cause a person of reasonable firmness present at the scene to fear for his personal safety, each of the persons using unlawful violence for the common purpose is guilty of riot.

(2) It is immaterial whether or not the 12 or more use or threaten unlawful violence simultaneously.

(3) The common purpose may be inferred from conduct.

(4) No person of reasonable firmness need actually be, or be likely to be, present at the scene.

(5) Riot may be committed in private as well as in public places.

(6) A person guilty of riot is liable on conviction on indictment to imprisonment for a term not exceeding ten years or a fine or both.

Violent disorder.

2.—(1) Where 3 or more persons who are present together use or threaten unlawful violence and the conduct of them (taken together) is such as would cause a person of reasonable firmness present at the scene to fear for his personal safety, each of the persons using or threatening unlawful violence is guilty of violent disorder.

(2) It is immaterial whether or not the 3 or more use or threaten unlawful violence simultaneously.

(3) No person of reasonable firmness need actually be, or be likely to be, present at the scene.

(4) Violent disorder may be committed in private as well as in public places.

(5) A person guilty of violent disorder is liable on conviction on indictment to imprisonment for a term not exceeding 5 years or a fine or both, or on summary conviction to imprisonment for a term not exceeding 6 months or a fine not exceeding the statutory maximum or both.

Affray.

3.—(1) A person is guilty of affray if he uses or threatens unlawful violence towards another and his conduct is such as would cause a person of reasonable firmness present at the scene to fear for his personal safety.

(2) Where 2 or more persons use or threaten the unlawful violence, it is the conduct of them taken together that must be considered for the purposes of subsection (1).

(3) For the purposes of this section a threat cannot be made by the use of words alone.

(4) No person of reasonable firmness need actually be, or be likely to be, present at the scene.

(5) Affray may be committed in private as well as in public places.

(6) A constable may arrest without warrant anyone he reasonably suspects is committing affray.

(7) A person guilty of affray is liable on conviction on indictment to imprisonment for a term not exceeding 3 years or a fine or both, or on summary conviction to imprisonment for a term not exceeding 6 months or a fine not exceeding the statutory maximum or both.

4.—(1) A person is guilty of an offence if he—   Fear or provocation of violence.

(a) uses towards another person threatening, abusive or insulting words or behaviour, or

(b) distributes or displays to another person any writing, sign or other visible representation which is threatening, abusive or insulting,

with intent to cause that person to believe that immediate unlawful violence will be used against him or another by any person, or to provoke the immediate use of unlawful violence by that person or another, or whereby that person is likely to believe that such violence will be used or it is likely that such violence will be provoked.

(2) An offence under this section may be committed in a public or a private place, except that no offence is committed where the words or behaviour are used, or the writing, sign or other visible representation is distributed or displayed, by a person inside a dwelling and the other person is also inside that or another dwelling.

(3) A constable may arrest without warrant anyone he reasonably suspects is committing an offence under this section.

(4) A person guilty of an offence under this section is liable on summary conviction to imprisonment for a term not exceeding 6 months or a fine not exceeding level 5 on the standard scale or both.

5.—(1) A person is guilty of an offence if he—   Harassment, alarm or distress.

(a) uses threatening, abusive or insulting words or behaviour, or disorderly behaviour, or

(b) displays any writing, sign or other visible representation which is threatening, abusive or insulting,

within the hearing or sight of a person likely to be caused harassment, alarm or distress thereby.

(2) An offence under this section may be committed in a public or a private place, except that no offence is committed

where the words or behaviour are used, or the writing, sign or other visible representation is displayed, by a person inside a dwelling and the other person is also inside that or another dwelling.

(3) It is a defence for the accused to prove—

(*a*) that he had no reason to believe that there was any person within hearing or sight who was likely to be caused harassment, alarm or distress, or

(*b*) that he was inside a dwelling and had no reason to believe that the words or behaviour used, or the writing, sign or other visible representation displayed, would be heard or seen by a person outside that or any other dwelling, or

(*c*) that his conduct was reasonable.

(4) A constable may arrest a person without warrant if—

(*a*) he engages in offensive conduct which the constable warns him to stop, and

(*b*) he engages in further offensive conduct immediately or shortly after the warning.

(5) In subsection (4) " offensive conduct " means conduct the constable reasonably suspects to constitute an offence under this section, and the conduct mentioned in paragraph (*a*) and the further conduct need not be of the same nature.

(6) A person guilty of an offence under this section is liable on summary conviction to a fine not exceeding level 3 on the standard scale.

Mental
element:
miscellaneous.
6.—(1) A person is guilty of riot only if he intends to use violence or is aware that his conduct may be violent.

(2) A person is guilty of violent disorder or affray only if he intends to use or threaten violence or is aware that his conduct may be violent or threaten violence.

(3) A person is guilty of an offence under section 4 only if he intends his words or behaviour, or the writing, sign or other visible representation, to be threatening, abusive or insulting, or is aware that it may be threatening, abusive or insulting.

(4) A person is guilty of an offence under section 5 only if he intends his words or behaviour, or the writing, sign or other visible representation, to be threatening, abusive or insulting, or is aware that it may be threatening, abusive or insulting or (as the case may be) he intends his behaviour to be or is aware that it may be disorderly.

(5) For the purposes of this section a person whose awareness is impaired by intoxication shall be taken to be aware of that of which he would be aware if not intoxicated, unless he shows

either that his intoxication was not self-induced or that it was caused solely by the taking or administration of a substance in the course of medical treatment.

(6) In subsection (5) " intoxication " means any intoxication, whether caused by drink, drugs or other means, or by a combination of means.

(7) Subsections (1) and (2) do not affect the determination for the purposes of riot or violent disorder of the number of persons who use or threaten violence.

7.—(1) No prosecution for an offence of riot or incitement to riot may be instituted except by or with the consent of the Director of Public Prosecutions. Procedure: miscellaneous.

(2) For the purposes of the rules against charging more than one offence in the same count or information, each of sections 1 to 5 creates one offence.

(3) If on the trial on indictment of a person charged with violent disorder or affray the jury find him not guilty of the offence charged, they may (without prejudice to section 6(3) of the Criminal Law Act 1967) find him guilty of an offence under section 4. 1967 c. 58.

(4) The Crown Court has the same powers and duties in relation to a person who is by virtue of subsection (3) convicted before it of an offence under section 4 as a magistrates' court would have on convicting him of the offence.

8. In this Part— Interpretation.

" dwelling " means any structure or part of a structure occupied as a person's home or as other living accommodation (whether the occupation is separate or shared with others) but does not include any part not so occupied, and for this purpose " structure " includes a tent, caravan, vehicle, vessel or other temporary or movable structure ;

" violence " means any violent conduct, so that—

(a) except in the context of affray, it includes violent conduct towards property as well as violent conduct towards persons, and

(b) it is not restricted to conduct causing or intended to cause injury or damage but includes any other violent conduct (for example, throwing at or towards a person a missile of a kind capable of causing injury which does not hit or falls short).

A 2

PART I
Offences
abolished.

9.—(1) The common law offences of riot, rout, unlawful assembly and affray are abolished.

(2) The offences under the following enactments are abolished—

1661 c. 5.

(a) section 1 of the Tumultuous Petitioning Act 1661 (presentation of petition to monarch or Parliament accompanied by excessive number of persons),

1793 c. 67.

(b) section 1 of the Shipping Offences Act 1793 (interference with operation of vessel by persons riotously assembled),

1817 c. 19.

(c) section 23 of the Seditious Meetings Act 1817 (prohibition of certain meetings within one mile of Westminster Hall when Parliament sitting), and

1936 c. 6.

(d) section 5 of the Public Order Act 1936 (conduct conducive to breach of the peace).

Construction
of other
instruments.
1886 c. 38.
1894 c. 60.
1906 c. 41.

10.—(1) In the Riot (Damages) Act 1886 and in section 515 of the Merchant Shipping Act 1894 (compensation for riot damage) " riotous " and " riotously " shall be construed in accordance with section 1 above.

(2) In Schedule 1 to the Marine Insurance Act 1906 (form and rules for the construction of certain insurance policies) " rioters " in rule 8 and " riot " in rule 10 shall, in the application of the rules to any policy taking effect on or after the coming into force of this section, be construed in accordance with section 1 above unless a different intention appears.

(3) " Riot " and cognate expressions in any enactment in force before the coming into force of this section (other than the enactments mentioned in subsections (1) and (2) above) shall be construed in accordance with section 1 above if they would have been construed in accordance with the common law offence of riot apart from this Part.

(4) Subject to subsections (1) to (3) above and unless a different intention appears, nothing in this Part affects the meaning of " riot " or any cognate expression in any enactment in force, or other instrument taking effect, before the coming into force of this section.

PART II

PROCESSIONS AND ASSEMBLIES

Advance notice
of public
processions.

11.—(1) Written notice shall be given in accordance with this section of any proposal to hold a public procession intended—

(a) to demonstrate support for or opposition to the views or actions of any person or body of persons, (*b*) to publicise a cause or campaign, or

(*c*) to mark or commemorate an event,

unless it is not reasonably practicable to give any advance notice of the procession.

(2) Subsection (1) does not apply where the procession is one commonly or customarily held in the police area (or areas) in which it is proposed to be held or is a funeral procession organised by a funeral director acting in the normal course of his business.

(3) The notice must specify the date when it is intended to hold the procession, the time when it is intended to start it, its proposed route, and the name and address of the person (or of one of the persons) proposing to organise it.

(4) Notice must be delivered to a police station—

(*a*) in the police area in which it is proposed the procession will start, or

(*b*) where it is proposed the procession will start in Scotland and cross into England, in the first police area in England on the proposed route.

(5) If delivered not less than 6 clear days before the date when the procession is intended to be held, the notice may be delivered by post by the recorded delivery service; but section 7 of the Interpretation Act 1978 (under which a document sent by post is 1978 c. 30. deemed to have been served when posted and to have been delivered in the ordinary course of post) does not apply.

(6) If not delivered in accordance with subsection (5), the notice must be delivered by hand not less than 6 clear days before the date when the procession is intended to be held or, if that is not reasonably practicable, as soon as delivery is reasonably practicable.

(7) Where a public procession is held, each of the persons organising it is guilty of an offence if—

(*a*) the requirements of this section as to notice have not been satisfied, or

(*b*) the date when it is held, the time when it starts, or its route, differs from the date, time or route specified in the notice.

(8) It is a defence for the accused to prove that he did not know of, and neither suspected nor had reason to suspect, the failure to satisfy the requirements or (as the case may be) the difference of date, time or route.

(9) To the extent that an alleged offence turns on a difference of date, time or route, it is a defence for the accused to prove that the difference arose from circumstances beyond his control

A 3

or from something done with the agreement of a police officer or by his direction.

(10) A person guilty of an offence under subsection (7) is liable on summary conviction to a fine not exceeding level 3 on the standard scale.

Imposing conditions on public processions.

12.—(1) If the senior police officer, having regard to the time or place at which and the circumstances in which any public procession is being held or is intended to be held and to its route or proposed route, reasonably believes that—

    (a) it may result in serious public disorder, serious damage to property or serious disruption to the life of the community, or

    (b) the purpose of the persons organising it is the intimidation of others with a view to compelling them not to do an act they have a right to do, or to do an act they have a right not to do,

he may give directions imposing on the persons organising or taking part in the procession such conditions as appear to him necessary to prevent such disorder, damage, disruption or intimidation, including conditions as to the route of the procession or prohibiting it from entering any public place specified in the directions.

(2) In subsection (1) " the senior police officer " means—

    (a) in relation to a procession being held, or to a procession intended to be held in a case where persons are assembling with a view to taking part in it, the most senior in rank of the police officers present at the scene, and

    (b) in relation to a procession intended to be held in a case where paragraph (a) does not apply, the chief officer of police.

(3) A direction given by a chief officer of police by virtue of subsection (2)(b) shall be given in writing.

(4) A person who organises a public procession and knowingly fails to comply with a condition imposed under this section is guilty of an offence, but it is a defence for him to prove that the failure arose from circumstances beyond his control.

(5) A person who takes part in a public procession and knowingly fails to comply with a condition imposed under this section is guilty of an offence, but it is a defence for him to prove that the failure arose from circumstances beyond his control.

(6) A person who incites another to commit an offence under subsection (5) is guilty of an offence.

(7) A constable in uniform may arrest without warrant anyone he reasonably suspects is committing an offence under subsection (4), (5) or (6).

(8) A person guilty of an offence under subsection (4) is liable on summary conviction to imprisonment for a term not exceeding 3 months or a fine not exceeding level 4 on the standard scale or both.

(9) A person guilty of an offence under subsection (5) is liable on summary conviction to a fine not exceeding level 3 on the standard scale.

(10) A person guilty of an offence under subsection (6) is liable on summary conviction to imprisonment for a term not exceeding 3 months or a fine not exceeding level 4 on the standard scale or both, notwithstanding section 45(3) of the Magistrates' Courts Act 1980 (inciter liable to same penalty as incited).

1980 c. 43.

(11) In Scotland this section applies only in relation to a procession being held, and to a procession intended to be held in a case where persons are assembling with a view to taking part in it.

13.—(1) If at any time the chief officer of police reasonably believes that, because of particular circumstances existing in any district or part of a district, the powers under section 12 will not be sufficient to prevent the holding of public processions in that district or part from resulting in serious public disorder, he shall apply to the council of the district for an order prohibiting for such period not exceeding 3 months as may be specified in the application the holding of all public processions (or of any class of public procession so specified) in the district or part concerned.

Prohibiting public processions.

(2) On receiving such an application, a council may with the consent of the Secretary of State make an order either in the terms of the application or with such modifications as may be approved by the Secretary of State.

(3) Subsection (1) does not apply in the City of London or the metropolitan police district.

(4) If at any time the Commissioner of Police for the City of London or the Commissioner of Police of the Metropolis reasonably believes that, because of particular circumstances existing in his police area or part of it, the powers under section 12 will not be sufficient to prevent the holding of public processions in that area or part from resulting in serious public disorder, he may with the consent of the Secretary of State make an order prohibiting for such period not exceeding 3 months as may be specified in the order the holding of all public processions (or

A 4

PART II

of any class of public procession so specified) in the area or part concerned.

(5) An order made under this section may be revoked or varied by a subsequent order made in the same way, that is, in accordance with subsections (1) and (2) or subsection (4), as the case may be.

(6) Any order under this section shall, if not made in writing, be recorded in writing as soon as practicable after being made.

(7) A person who organises a public procession the holding of which he knows is prohibited by virtue of an order under this section is guilty of an offence.

(8) A person who takes part in a public procession the holding of which he knows is prohibited by virtue of an order under this section is guilty of an offence.

(9) A person who incites another to commit an offence under subsection (8) is guilty of an offence.

(10) A constable in uniform may arrest without warrant anyone he reasonably suspects is committing an offence under subsection (7), (8) or (9).

(11) A person guilty of an offence under subsection (7) is liable on summary conviction to imprisonment for a term not exceeding 3 months or a fine not exceeding level 4 on the standard scale or both.

(12) A person guilty of an offence under subsection (8) is liable on summary conviction to a fine not exceeding level 3 on the standard scale.

1980 c. 43.

(13) A person guilty of an offence under subsection (9) is liable on summary conviction to imprisonment for a term not exceeding 3 months or a fine not exceeding level 4 on the standard scale or both, notwithstanding section 45(3) of the Magistrates' Courts Act 1980.

Imposing conditions on public assemblies.

14.—(1) If the senior police officer, having regard to the time or place at which and the circumstances in which any public assembly is being held or is intended to be held, reasonably believes that—

(a) it may result in serious public disorder, serious damage to property or serious disruption to the life of the community, or

(b) the purpose of the persons organising it is the intimidation of others with a view to compelling them not to do an act they have a right to do, or to do an act they have a right not to do,

he may give directions imposing on the persons organising or taking part in the assembly such conditions as to the place at which the assembly may be (or continue to be) held, its maximum duration, or the maximum number of persons who may constitute it, as appear to him necessary to prevent such disorder, damage, disruption or intimidation.

(2) In subsection (1) " the senior police officer " means—

(a) in relation to an assembly being held, the most senior in rank of the police officers present at the scene, and

(b) in relation to an assembly intended to be held, the chief officer of police.

(3) A direction given by a chief officer of police by virtue of subsection (2)(b) shall be given in writing.

(4) A person who organises a public assembly and knowingly fails to comply with a condition imposed under this section is guilty of an offence, but it is a defence for him to prove that the failure arose from circumstances beyond his control.

(5) A person who takes part in a public assembly and knowingly fails to comply with a condition imposed under this section is guilty of an offence, but it is a defence for him to prove that the failure arose from circumstances beyond his control.

(6) A person who incites another to commit an offence under subsection (5) is guilty of an offence.

(7) A constable in uniform may arrest without warrant anyone he reasonably suspects is committing an offence under subsection (4), (5) or (6).

(8) A person guilty of an offence under subsection (4) is liable on summary conviction to imprisonment for a term not exceeding 3 months or a fine not exceeding level 4 on the standard scale or both.

(9) A person guilty of an offence under subsection (5) is liable on summary conviction to a fine not exceeding level 3 on the standard scale.

(10) A person guilty of an offence under subsection (6) is liable on summary conviction to imprisonment for a term not exceeding 3 months or a fine not exceeding level 4 on the standard scale or both, notwithstanding section 45(3) of the Magistrates' Courts Act 1980. 1980 c. 43.

15.—(1) The chief officer of police may delegate, to such Delegation. extent and subject to such conditions as he may specify, any of his functions under sections 12 to 14 to a deputy or assistant chief constable; and references in those sections to the person delegating shall be construed accordingly.

(2) Subsection (1) shall have effect in the City of London and the metropolitan police district as if " a deputy or assistant chief constable " read " an assistant commissioner of police ".

A 5

16. In this Part—

"the City of London" means the City as defined for the purposes of the Acts relating to the City of London police;

"the metropolitan police district" means that district as defined in section 76 of the London Government Act 1963;

"public assembly" means an assembly of 20 or more persons in a public place which is wholly or partly open to the air;

"public place" means—

(a) any highway, or in Scotland any road within the meaning of the Roads (Scotland) Act 1984, and

(b) any place to which at the material time the public or any section of the public has access, on payment or otherwise, as of right or by virtue of express or implied permission;

"public procession" means a procession in a public place.

PART III

RACIAL HATRED

Meaning of "racial hatred"

17. In this Part "racial hatred" means hatred against a group of persons in Great Britain defined by reference to colour, race, nationality (including citizenship) or ethnic or national origins.

Acts intended or likely to stir up racial hatred

18.—(1) A person who uses threatening, abusive or insulting words or behaviour, or displays any written material which is threatening, abusive or insulting, is guilty of an offence if—

(a) he intends thereby to stir up racial hatred, or

(b) having regard to all the circumstances racial hatred is likely to be stirred up thereby.

(2) An offence under this section may be committed in a public or a private place, except that no offence is committed where the words or behaviour are used, or the written material is displayed, by a person inside a dwelling and are not heard or seen except by other persons in that or another dwelling.

(3) A constable may arrest without warrant anyone he reasonably suspects is committing an offence under this section.

(4) In proceedings for an offence under this section it is a defence for the accused to prove that he was inside a dwelling and had no reason to believe that the words or behaviour used,

or the written material displayed, would be heard or seen by a   PART III
person outside that or any other dwelling.

(5) A person who is not shown to have intended to stir up
racial hatred is not guilty of an offence under this section if he
did not intend his words or behaviour, or the written material,
to be, and was not aware that it might be, threatening, abusive
or insulting.

(6) This section does not apply to words or behaviour used, or
written material displayed, solely for the purpose of being
included in a programme broadcast or included in a cable programme service.

19.—(1) A person who publishes or distributes written material   Publishing or
which is threatening, abusive or insulting is guilty of an offence   distributing
if—   written
material.

(a) he intends thereby to stir up racial hatred, or

(b) having regard to all the circumstances racial hatred is
likely to be stirred up thereby.

(2) In proceedings for an offence under this section it is a
defence for an accused who is not shown to have intended to stir
up racial hatred to prove that he was not aware of the content of
the material and did not suspect, and had no reason to suspect,
that it was threatening, abusive or insulting.

(3) References in this Part to the publication or distribution of
written material are to its publication or distribution to the public
or a section of the public.

20.—(1) If a public performance of a play is given which   Public
involves the use of threatening, abusive or insulting words or   performance
behaviour, any person who presents or directs the performance   of play.
is guilty of an offence if—

(a) he intends thereby to stir up racial hatred, or

(b) having regard to all the circumstances (and, in particular, taking the performance as a whole) racial hatred is
likely to be stirred up thereby.

(2) If a person presenting or directing the performance is not
shown to have intended to stir up racial hatred, it is a defence
for him to prove—

(a) that he did not know and had no reason to suspect that
the performance would involve the use of the offending
words or behaviour, or

(b) that he did not know and had no reason to suspect
that the offending words or behaviour were threatening, abusive or insulting, or

(c) that he did not know and had no reason to suspect that the circumstances in which the performance would be given would be such that racial hatred would be likely to be stirred up.

(3) This section does not apply to a performance given solely or primarily for one or more of the following purposes—

(a) rehearsal,

(b) making a recording of the performance, or

(c) enabling the performance to be broadcast or included in a cable programme service ;

but if it is proved that the performance was attended by persons other than those directly connected with the giving of the performance or the doing in relation to it of the things mentioned in paragraph (b) or (c), the performance shall, unless the contrary is shown, be taken not to have been given solely or primarily for the purposes mentioned above.

(4) For the purposes of this section—

(a) a person shall not be treated as presenting a performance of a play by reason only of his taking part in it as a performer,

(b) a person taking part as a performer in a performance directed by another shall be treated as a person who directed the performance if without reasonable excuse he performs otherwise than in accordance with that person's direction, and

(c) a person shall be taken to have directed a performance of a play given under his direction notwithstanding that he was not present during the performance ;

and a person shall not be treated as aiding or abetting the commission of an offence under this section by reason only of his taking part in a performance as a performer.

(5) In this section " play " and " public performance " have the same meaning as in the Theatres Act 1968.

1968 c. 54.

(6) The following provisions of the Theatres Act 1968 apply in relation to an offence under this section as they apply to an offence under section 2 of that Act—

section 9 (script as evidence of what was performed),

section 10 (power to make copies of script),

section 15 (powers of entry and inspection).

Distributing, showing or playing a recording.

21.—(1) A person who distributes, or shows or plays, a recording of visual images or sounds which are threatening, abusive or insulting is guilty of an offence if—

(a) he intends thereby to stir up racial hatred, or

(b) having regard to all the circumstances racial hatred is likely to be stirred up thereby.

(2) In this Part " recording " means any record from which
visual images or sounds may, by any means, be reproduced ;
and references to the distribution, showing or playing of a
recording are to its distribution, showing or playing to the public
or a section of the public.

(3) In proceedings for an offence under this section it is a
defence for an accused who is not shown to have intended to
stir up racial hatred to prove that he was not aware of the
content of the recording and did not suspect, and had no reason
to suspect, that it was threatening, abusive or insulting.

(4) This section does not apply to the showing or playing of a
recording solely for the purpose of enabling the recording to be
broadcast or included in a cable programme service.

22.—(1) If a programme involving threatening, abusive or Broadcasting
insulting visual images or sounds is broadcast, or included in or including
a cable programme service, each of the persons mentioned in programme
subsection (2) is guilty of an offence if—   in cable programme service.

  (*a*) he intends thereby to stir up racial hatred, or

  (*b*) having regard to all the circumstances racial hatred is
    likely to be stirred up thereby.

(2) The persons are—

  (*a*) the person providing the broadcasting or cable pro-
    gramme service,

  (*b*) any person by whom the programme is produced or
    directed, and

  (*c*) any person by whom offending words or behaviour are
    used.

(3) If the person providing the service, or a person by whom
the programme was produced or directed, is not shown to have
intended to stir up racial hatred, it is a defence for him to prove
that—

  (*a*) he did not know and had no reason to suspect that the
    programme would involve the offending material, and

  (*b*) having regard to the circumstances in which the pro-
    gramme was broadcast, or included in a cable pro-
    gramme service, it was not reasonably practicable for
    him to secure the removal of the material.

(4) It is a defence for a person by whom the programme was
produced or directed who is not shown to have intended to stir
up racial hatred to prove that he did not know and had no
reason to suspect—

  (*a*) that the programme would be broadcast or included in
    a cable programme service, or

(*b*) that the circumstances in which the programme would be broadcast or so included would be such that racial hatred would be likely to be stirred up.

(5) It is a defence for a person by whom offending words or behaviour were used and who is not shown to have intended to stir up racial hatred to prove that he did not know and had no reason to suspect—

(*a*) that a programme involving the use of the offending material would be broadcast or included in a cable programme service, or

(*b*) that the circumstances in which a programme involving the use of the offending material would be broadcast, or so included, or in which a programme broadcast or so included would involve the use of the offending material, would be such that racial hatred would be likely to be stirred up.

(6) A person who is not shown to have intended to stir up racial hatred is not guilty of an offence under this section if he did not know, and had no reason to suspect, that the offending material was threatening, abusive or insulting.

(7) This section does not apply—

(*a*) to the broadcasting of a programme by the British Broadcasting Corporation or the Independent Broadcasting Authority, or

(*b*) to the inclusion of a programme in a cable programme service by the reception and immediate re-transmission of a broadcast by either of those authorities.

1984 c. 46.

(8) The following provisions of the Cable and Broadcasting Act 1984 apply to an offence under this section as they apply to a " relevant offence " as defined in section 33(2) of that Act—

section 33 (scripts as evidence),

section 34 (power to make copies of scripts and records),

section 35 (availability of visual and sound records) ;

and sections 33 and 34 of that Act apply to an offence under this section in connection with the broadcasting of a programme as they apply to an offence in connection with the inclusion of a programme in a cable programme service.

Racially inflammatory material

Possession of racially inflammatory material.

23.—(1) A person who has in his possession written material which is threatening, abusive or insulting, or a recording of visual images or sounds which are threatening, abusive or insulting, with a view to—

(*a*) in the case of written material, its being displayed, published, distributed, broadcast or included in a cable programme service, whether by himself or another, or

(*b*) in the case of a recording, its being distributed, shown,   PART III
played, broadcast or included in a cable programme
service, whether by himself or another,

is guilty of an offence if he intends racial hatred to be stirred up
thereby or, having regard to all the circumstances, racial hatred
is likely to be stirred up thereby.

(2) For this purpose regard shall be had to such display, publication, distribution, showing, playing, broadcasting or inclusion in a cable programme service as he has, or it may reasonably
be inferred that he has, in view.

(3) In proceedings for an offence under this section it is a
defence for an accused who is not shown to have intended to
stir up racial hatred to prove that he was not aware of the content
of the written material or recording and did not suspect, and
had no reason to suspect, that it was threatening, abusive or
insulting.

(4) This section does not apply to the possession of written
material or a recording by or on behalf of the British Broadcasting Corporation or the Independent Broadcasting Authority
or with a view to its being broadcast by either of those
authorities.

24.—(1) If in England and Wales a justice of the peace is Powers of entry
satisfied by information on oath laid by a constable that there and search.
are reasonable grounds for suspecting that a person has possession of written material or a recording in contravention of
section 23, the justice may issue a warrant under his hand
authorising any constable to enter and search the premises
where it is suspected the material or recording is situated.

(2) If in Scotland a sheriff or justice of the peace is satisfied
by evidence on oath that there are reasonable grounds for
suspecting that a person has possession of written material or a
recording in contravention of section 23, the sheriff or justice
may issue a warrant authorising any constable to enter and
search the premises where it is suspected the material or recording is situated.

(3) A constable entering or searching premises in pursuance
of a warrant issued under this section may use reasonable force
if necessary.

(4) In this section " premises " means any place and, in
particular, includes—

    (*a*) any vehicle, vessel, aircraft or hovercraft,

    (*b*) any offshore installation as defined in section 1(3) (*b*)
         of the Mineral Workings (Offshore Installations) Act 1971 c. 61.
         1971, and

    (*c*) any tent or movable structure.

25.—(1) A court by or before which a person is convicted of—

 (a) an offence under section 18 relating to the display of written material, or

 (b) an offence under section 19, 21 or 23,

shall order to be forfeited any written material or recording produced to the court and shown to its satisfaction to be written material or a recording to which the offence relates.

(2) An order made under this section shall not take effect—

 (a) in the case of an order made in proceedings in England and Wales, until the expiry of the ordinary time within which an appeal may be instituted or, where an appeal is duly instituted, until it is finally decided or abandoned ;

 (b) in the case of an order made in proceedings in Scotland, until the expiration of the time within which, by virtue of any statute, an appeal may be instituted or, where such an appeal is duly instituted, until the appeal is finally decided or abandoned.

(3) For the purposes of subsection (2)(a)—

 (a) an application for a case stated or for leave to appeal shall be treated as the institution of an appeal, and

 (b) where a decision on appeal is subject to a further appeal, the appeal is not finally determined until the expiry of the ordinary time within which a further appeal may be instituted or, where a further appeal is duly instituted, until the further appeal is finally decided or abandoned.

(4) For the purposes of subsection (2)(b) the lodging of an application for a stated case or note of appeal against sentence shall be treated as the institution of an appeal.

Supplementary provisions

26.—(1) Nothing in this Part applies to a fair and accurate report of proceedings in Parliament.

(2) Nothing in this Part applies to a fair and accurate report of proceedings publicly heard before a court or tribunal exercising judicial authority where the report is published contemporaneously with the proceedings or, if it is not reasonably practicable or would be unlawful to publish a report of them contemporaneously, as soon as publication is reasonably practicable and lawful.

27.—(1) No proceedings for an offence under this Part may be instituted in England and Wales except by or with the consent of the Attorney General.

(2) For the purposes of the rules in England and Wales against charging more than one offence in the same count or information, each of sections 18 to 23 creates one offence.

(3) A person guilty of an offence under this Part is liable—

(a) on conviction on indictment to imprisonment for a term not exceeding two years or a fine or both ;

(b) on summary conviction to imprisonment for a term not exceeding six months or a fine not exceeding the statutory maximum or both.

28.—(1) Where a body corporate is guilty of an offence under this Part and it is shown that the offence was committed with the consent or connivance of a director, manager, secretary or other similar officer of the body, or a person purporting to act in any such capacity, he as well as the body corporate is guilty of the offence and liable to be proceeded against and punished accordingly. Offences by corporations.

(2) Where the affairs of a body corporate are managed by its members, subsection (1) applies in relation to the acts and defaults of a member in connection with his functions of management as it applies to a director.

29. In this Part— Interpretation.

" broadcast " means broadcast by wireless telegraphy (within the meaning of the Wireless Telegraphy Act 1949) for general reception, whether by way of sound broadcasting or television ; 1949 c. 54.

" cable programme service " has the same meaning as in the Cable and Broadcasting Act 1984 ; 1984 c. 46.

" distribute ", and related expressions, shall be construed in accordance with section 19(3) (written material) and section 21(2) (recordings) ;

" dwelling " means any structure or part of a structure occupied as a person's home or other living accommodation (whether the occupation is separate or shared with others) but does not include any part not so occupied, and for this purpose " structure " includes a tent, caravan, vehicle, vessel or other temporary or movable structure ;

" programme " means any item which is broadcast or included in a cable programme service ;

" publish ", and related expressions, in relation to written material, shall be construed in accordance with section 19 (3);

" racial hatred " has the meaning given by section 17 ;

"recording" has the meaning given by section 21(2), and "play" and "show", and related expressions, in relation to a recording, shall be construed in accordance with that provision;

"written material" includes any sign or other visible representation.

Part IV

Exclusion Orders

Exclusion orders.

30.—(1) A court by or before which a person is convicted of an offence to which section 31 applies may make an order (an exclusion order) prohibiting him from entering any premises for the purpose of attending any prescribed football match there.

(2) No exclusion order may be made unless the court is satisfied that making such an order in relation to the accused would help to prevent violence or disorder at or in connection with prescribed football matches.

(3) An exclusion order may only be made—

(a) in addition to a sentence imposed in respect of the offence of which the accused is convicted, or

(b) in addition to a probation order or an order discharging him absolutely or conditionally.

1973 c. 62.

(4) An exclusion order may be made as mentioned in subsection (3)(b) notwithstanding anything in sections 2, 7 and 13 of the Powers of Criminal Courts Act 1973 (which relate to orders there mentioned and their effect).

Offences connected with football.

31.—(1) This section applies to any offence which fulfils one or more of the following three conditions.

(2) The first condition is that the offence was committed during any period relevant to a prescribed football match (as determined under subsections (6) to (8)), while the accused was at, or was entering or leaving or trying to enter or leave, the football ground concerned.

(3) The second condition is that the offence—

(a) involved the use or threat of violence by the accused towards another person and was committed while one or each of them was on a journey to or from an association football match,

(b) involved the use or threat of violence towards property and was committed while the accused was on such a journey, or

(c) was committed under section 5 or Part III while the accused was on such a journey.

(4) The third condition is that the offence was committed under section 1(3) or (4) or 1A(3) or (4) of the Sporting Events (Control of Alcohol etc.) Act 1985 (alcohol on journeys to or from certain sporting events) and the designated sporting event concerned was an association football match.

(5) For the purposes of subsection (3) a person's journey includes breaks (including overnight breaks).

(6) The period beginning 2 hours before the start of the match or (if earlier) 2 hours before the time at which it is advertised to start, and ending 1 hour after the end of it, is a period relevant to it.

(7) Where the match is advertised to start at a particular time on a particular day and is postponed to a later day, the period in the advertised day beginning 2 hours before and ending 1 hour after that time is also a period relevant to it.

(8) Where the match is advertised to start at a particular time on a particular day and does not take place, the period in that day beginning 2 hours before and ending 1 hour after that time is a period relevant to it.

32.—(1) An exclusion order shall have effect for such period Effect of as is specified in the order. order.

(2) The period shall be not less than three months or, in the case of a person already subject to an exclusion order, not less than three months plus the unexpired period of the earlier order or, if there is more than one earlier order, of the most recent order.

(3) A person who enters premises in breach of an exclusion order is guilty of an offence and liable on summary conviction to imprisonment for a term not exceeding 1 month or a fine not exceeding level 3 on the standard scale or both.

(4) A constable who reasonably suspects that a person has entered premises in breach of an exclusion order may arrest him without warrant.

33.—(1) A person in relation to whom an exclusion order has Application had effect for at least one year may apply to the court by which to terminate it was made to terminate it. order.

(2) On such an application the court may, having regard to the person's character, his conduct since the order was made, the nature of the offence which led to it and any other circumstances of the case, either by order terminate the order (as from a date specified in the terminating order) or refuse the application.

PART IV

(3) Where an application under this section is refused, a further application in respect of the exclusion order shall not be entertained if made within the period of six months beginning with the day of the refusal.

(4) The court may order the applicant to pay all or any part of the costs of an application under this section.

(5) In the case of an exclusion order made by a magistrates' court, the reference in subsection (1) to the court by which it was made includes a reference to any magistrates' court acting for the same petty sessions area as that court.

1980 c. 43.

(6) Section 63(2) of the Magistrates' Courts Act 1980 (power to suspend or rescind orders) does not apply to an exclusion order.

Information.

34.—(1) Where a court makes an exclusion order, the clerk of the court (in the case of a magistrates' court) or the appropriate officer (in the case of the Crown Court)—

(a) shall give a copy of it to the person to whom it relates,

(b) shall (as soon as reasonably practicable) send a copy of it to the chief officer of police for the police area in which the offence leading to the order was committed, and

(c) shall (as soon as reasonably practicable) send a copy of it to any prescribed person.

(2) Where a court terminates an exclusion order under section 28, the clerk of the court (in the case of a magistrates' court) or the appropriate officer (in the case of the Crown Court)—

(a) shall give a copy of the terminating order to the person to whom the exclusion order relates,

(b) shall (as soon as reasonably practicable) send a copy of the terminating order to the chief officer of police for the police area in which the offence leading to the exclusion order was committed, and

(c) shall (as soon as reasonably practicable) send a copy of the terminating order to any prescribed person.

1980 c. 43.

(3) References in this section to the clerk of a magistrates' court shall be construed in accordance with section 141 of the Magistrates' Courts Act 1980, reading references to that Act as references to this section.

(4) In this section " prescribed " means prescribed by order made by the Secretary of State.

(5) The power to make an order under this section shall be exercisable by statutory instrument subject to annulment in pursuance of a resolution of either House of Parliament.

35.—(1) The court by which an exclusion order is made may make an order which—

    (*a*) requires a constable to take a photograph of the person to whom the exclusion order relates or to cause such a photograph to be taken, and

    (*b*) requires that person to go to a specified police station not later than 7 clear days after the day on which the order under this section is made, and at a specified time of day or between specified times of day, in order to have his photograph taken.

PART IV
Photographs.

(2) In subsection (1) " specified " means specified in the order made under this section.

(3) No order may be made under this section unless an application to make it is made to the court by or on behalf of the person who is the prosecutor in respect of the offence leading to the exclusion order.

(4) If the person to whom the exclusion order relates fails to comply with an order under this section a constable may arrest him without warrant in order that his photograph may be taken.

36.—(1) In this Part " prescribed football match " means an association football match of any description prescribed by order made by the Secretary of State.

Prescribed
football
matches.

(2) The power to make an order under this section shall be exercisable by statutory instrument subject to annulment in pursuance of a resolution of either House of Parliament.

37.—(1) The Secretary of State may by order provide for sections 30 to 35 to apply as if—

    (*a*) any reference to an association football match included a reference to a sporting event of a kind specified in the order, and

    (*b*) any reference to a prescribed football match included a reference to such a sporting event of a description specified in the order.

Extension
to other
sporting
events.

(2) An order under subsection (1) may make such modifications of those sections, as they apply by virtue of the order, as the Secretary of State thinks fit.

(3) The power to make an order under this section shall be exercisable by statutory instrument, and no such order shall be made unless a draft of the order has been laid before and approved by resolution of each House of Parliament.

PART V

MISCELLANEOUS AND GENERAL

Contamination
of or
interference
with goods
with intention
of causing
public alarm or
anxiety, etc.

38.—(1) It is an offence for a person, with the intention—

(a) of causing public alarm or anxiety, or

(b) of causing injury to members of the public consuming or using the goods, or

(c) of causing economic loss to any person by reason of the goods being shunned by members of the public, or

(d) of causing economic loss to any person by reason of steps taken to avoid any such alarm or anxiety, injury or loss,

to contaminate or interfere with goods, or make it appear that goods have been contaminated or interfered with, or to place goods which have been contaminated or interfered with, or which appear to have been contaminated or interfered with, in a place where goods of that description are consumed, used, sold or otherwise supplied.

(2) It is also an offence for a person, with any such intention as is mentioned in paragraph (a), (c) *or* (d) of subsection (1), to threaten that he or another will do, or to claim that he or another has done, any of the acts mentioned in that subsection.

(3) It is an offence for a person to be in possession of any of the following articles with a view to the commission of an offence under subsection (1)—

(a) materials to be used for contaminating or interfering with goods or making it appear that goods have been contaminated or interfered with, or

(b) goods which have been contaminated or interfered with, or which appear to have been contaminated or interfered with.

(4) A person guilty of an offence under this section is liable—

(a) on conviction on indictment to imprisonment for a term not exceeding 10 years or a fine or both, or

(b) on summary conviction to imprisonment for a term not exceeding six months or a fine not exceeding the statutory maximum or both.

(5) In this section "goods" includes substances whether natural or manufactured and whether or not incorporated in or mixed with other goods.

(6) The reference in subsection (2) to a person claiming that certain acts have been committed does not include a person who in good faith reports or warns that such acts have been, or appear to have been, committed.

39.—(1) If the senior police officer reasonably believes that   PART V
two or more persons have entered land as trespassers and are Power to direct
present there with the common purpose of residing there for trespassers to
any period, that reasonable steps have been taken by or on leave land.
behalf of the occupier to ask them to leave and—

    (*a*) that any of those persons has caused damage to pro-
        perty on the land or used threatening, abusive or
        insulting words or behaviour towards the occupier, a
        member of his family or an employee or agent of his,
        or

    (*b*) that those persons have between them brought twelve
        or more vehicles on to the land,

he may direct those persons, or any of them, to leave the land.

(2) If a person knowing that such a direction has been given
which applies to him—

    (*a*) fails to leave the land as soon as reasonably practicable,
        or

    (*b*) having left again enters the land as a trespasser within
        the period of three months beginning with the day on
        which the direction was given,

he commits an offence and is liable on summary conviction to
imprisonment for a term not exceeding three months or a fine
not exceeding level 4 on the standard scale, or both.

(3) A constable in uniform who reasonably suspects that a
person is committing an offence under this section may arrest
him without warrant.

(4) In proceedings for an offence under this section it is a
defence for the accused to show—

    (*a*) that his original entry on the land was not as a tres-
        passer, or

    (*b*) that he had a reasonable excuse for failing to leave the
        land as soon as reasonably practicable or, as the case
        may be, for again entering the land as a trespasser.

(5) In this section—

    " land " does not include—

        (*a*) buildings other than—

            (i) agricultural buildings within the meaning of
               section 26(4) of the General Rate Act 1967, 1967 c. 9.
               or

            (ii) scheduled monuments within the meaning of
               the Ancient Monuments and Archaeological 1979 c. 46.
               Areas Act 1979 ;

        (*b*) land forming part of a highway ;

" occupier " means the person entitled to possession of the land by virtue of an estate or interest held by him ;

" property " means property within the meaning of section 10(1) of the Criminal Damage Act 1971 ;

" senior police officer " means the most senior in rank of the police officers present at the scene ;

" trespasser ", in relation to land, means a person who is a trespasser as against the occupier of the land ;

" vehicle " includes a caravan as defined in section 29(1) of the Caravan Sites and Control of Development Act 1960 ;

and a person may be regarded for the purposes of this section as having the purpose of residing in a place notwithstanding that he has a home elsewhere.

40.—(1) Schedule 1, which amends the Sporting Events (Control of Alcohol etc.) Act 1985 and Part V of the Criminal Justice (Scotland) Act 1980, shall have effect.

(2) Schedule 2, which contains miscellaneous and consequential amendments, shall have effect.

(3) The enactments mentioned in Schedule 3 (which include enactments related to the subject matter of this Act but already obsolete or unnecessary) are repealed to the extent specified in column 3.

(4) Nothing in this Act affects the common law powers in England and Wales to deal with or prevent a breach of the peace.

(5) As respects Scotland, nothing in this Act affects any power of a constable under any rule of law.

41.—(1) This Act shall come into force on such day as the Secretary of State may appoint by order made by statutory instrument, and different days may be appointed for different provisions or different purposes.

(2) Nothing in a provision of this Act applies in relation to an offence committed or act done before the provision comes into force.

(3) Where a provision of this Act comes into force for certain purposes only, the references in subsection (2) to the provision are references to it so far as it relates to those purposes.

42.—(1) The provisions of this Act extend to England and Wales except so far as they—

    (*a*) amend or repeal an enactment which does not so extend, or

(b) relate to the extent of provisions to Scotland or Northern   PART V
    Ireland.

(2) The following provisions of this Act extend to Scotland—
    in Part I, section 9(2) except paragraph (a) ;
    in Part II, sections 12 and 14 to 16 ;
    Part III ;
    Part V, except sections 38, 39, 40(4), subsections (1) and (3)
        of this section and any provision amending or repealing
        an enactment which does not extend to Scotland.

(3) The following provisions of this Act extend to Northern
Ireland—
    sections 38, 41, this subsection, section 43 and paragraph
        6 of Schedule 2.

43. This Act may be cited as the Public Order Act 1986.   Short title.

SCHEDULES

SCHEDULE 1

SPORTING EVENTS

PART I

ENGLAND AND WALES

Introduction

1. The Sporting Events (Control of Alcohol etc.) Act 1985 shall be amended as mentioned in this Part.

Vehicles

2. The following shall be inserted after section 1 (offences in connection with alcohol on coaches and trains)—

"Alcohol on certain other vehicles.

1A.—(1) This section applies to a motor vehicle which—

    (*a*) is not a public service vehicle but is adapted to carry more than 8 passengers, and

    (*b*) is being used for the principal purpose of carrying two or more passengers for the whole or part of a journey to or from a designated sporting event.

(2) A person who knowingly causes or permits intoxicating liquor to be carried on a motor vehicle to which this section applies is guilty of an offence—

    (*a*) if he is its driver, or

    (*b*) if he is not its driver but is its keeper, the servant or agent of its keeper, a person to whom it is made available (by hire, loan or otherwise) by its keeper or the keeper's servant or agent, or the servant or agent of a person to whom it is so made available.

(3) A person who has intoxicating liquor in his possession while on a motor vehicle to which this section applies is guilty of an offence.

(4) A person who is drunk on a motor vehicle to which this section applies is guilty of an offence.

(5) In this section—

"keeper", in relation to a vehicle, means the person having the duty to take out a licence for it under section 1(1) of the Vehicles (Excise) Act 1971,

"motor vehicle" means a mechanically propelled vehicle intended or adapted for use on roads, and

" public service vehicle " has the same meaning as in   Sch. 1
the Public Passenger Vehicles Act 1981.".   1981 c. 14.

Fireworks etc.

3. The following shall be inserted after section 2 (offences in connection with alcohol, containers etc. at sports grounds)—

" Fireworks   2A.—(1) A person is guilty of an offence if he has an
etc.   article or substance to which this section applies in his
possession—

> (*a*) at any time during the period of a designated
> sporting event when he is in any area of a
> designated sports ground from which the event
> may be directly viewed, or

> (*b*) while entering or trying to enter a designated
> sports ground at any time during the period of a
> designated sporting event at the ground.

(2) It is a defence for the accused to prove that he
had possession with lawful authority.

(3) This section applies to any article or substance
whose main purpose is the emission of a flare for purposes
of illuminating or signalling (as opposed to igniting or
heating) or the emission of smoke or a visible gas ; and
in particular it applies to distress flares, fog signals, and
pellets and capsules intended to be used as fumigators
or for testing pipes, but not to matches, cigarette lighters
or heaters.

(4) This section also applies to any article which is a
firework.".

Licensing etc.

4. The following shall be inserted after section 5—

" Private   5A.—(1) In relation to a room in a designated sports
facilities for   ground—
viewing
events.

> (*a*) from which designated sporting events may be
> directly viewed, and

> (*b*) to which the general public are not admitted,

sections 2(1) (*a*) and 3(1) (*a*) of this Act have effect with
the substitution for the reference to the period of a designated sporting event of a reference to the restricted period
defined below.

(2) Subject to any order under subsection (3) below,
the restricted period of a designated sporting event for the
purposes of this section is the period beginning 15 minutes
before the start of the event or (if earlier) 15 minutes before
the time at which it is advertised to start and ending 15
minutes after the end of the event, but—

> (*a*) where an event advertised to start at a particular
> time on a particular day is postponed to a later

SCH. 1

day, the restricted period includes the period in the day on which it is advertised to take place beginning 15 minutes before and ending 15 minutes after that time, and

(b) where an event advertised to start at a particular time on a particular day does not take place, the period is the period referred to in paragraph (a) above.

(3) The Secretary of State may by order provide, in relation to all designated sporting events or in relation to such descriptions of event as are specified in the order—

(a) that the restricted period shall be such period, shorter than that mentioned in subsection (2) above, as may be specified in the order, or

(b) that there shall be no restricted period.

(4) An order under this section shall be made by statutory instrument which shall be subject to annulment in pursuance of a resolution of either House of Parliament.

Occasional licences.

5B.—(1) An occasional licence which is in force for any place situated in the area of a designated sports ground, and which would (apart from this section) authorise the sale of intoxicating liquor at the place during the whole or part of the period of a designated sporting event at the ground, shall not authorise such sale.

(2) Where the sale of intoxicating liquor would (apart from this section) be authorised by an occasional licence, its holder is guilty of an offence if he sells or authorises the sale of such liquor and by virtue of this section the licence does not authorise the sale.

(3) A person is guilty of an offence if he consumes intoxicating liquor at a place, or takes such liquor from a place, at a time when an occasional licence which would (apart from this section) authorise the sale of the liquor at the place does not do so by virtue of this section.

Clubs.

1964 c. 26.

5C.—(1) Subsections (3) and (5) of section 39 of the Licensing Act 1964 (clubs), and subsection (4) of that section as it applies to subsection (3), shall not apply as regards the supply of intoxicating liquor in the area of a designated sports ground during the period of a designated sporting event at the ground or as regards the keeping of intoxicating liquor for such supply; but subsections (2) to (5) below shall apply.

(2) During the period of such an event at the ground, intoxicating liquor shall not be supplied by or on behalf of a registered club to a member or guest in the area of the ground except at premises in respect of which the club is registered.

(3) A person supplying or authorising the supply of intoxicating liquor in contravention of subsection (2) above is guilty of an offence.

(4) A person who, during the period of such an event, obtains or consumes intoxicating liquor supplied in contravention of subsection (2) above is guilty of an offence.

(5) If intoxicating liquor is kept in any premises or place by or on behalf of a club for supply to members or their guests in contravention of subsection (2) above, every officer of the club is guilty of an offence unless he shows that it was so kept without his knowledge or consent.

Non-retail sales.

5D.—(1) During the period of a designated sporting event at a designated sports ground, intoxicating liquor shall not be sold in the area of the ground except by sale by retail.

(2) A person selling or authorising the sale of intoxicating liquor in contravention of subsection (1) above is guilty of an offence.

(3) A person who, during the period of such an event, obtains or consumes intoxicating liquor sold in contravention of subsection (1) above is guilty of an offence.".

Supplementary

5. In sections 2 and 3, after subsection (1) insert—

"(1A) Subsection (1)(a) above has effect subject to section 5A(1) of this Act."

6. In section 7(3) (power to stop and search vehicles), after "public service vehicle (within the meaning of section 1 of this Act)" insert "or a motor vehicle to which section 1A of this Act applies".

7.—(1) Section 8 (penalties) shall be amended as follows.

(2) In paragraph (a) after "1(2)" there shall be inserted "or 1A(2)".

(3) In paragraph (b) after "1(3)" there shall be inserted ", 1A(3)", after "2(1)" there shall be inserted ", 2A(1)" and after "3(10)" there shall be inserted ", 5B(2), 5C(3), 5D(2)".

(4) In paragraph (c) after "1(4)" there shall be inserted ", 1A(4)".

(5) At the end there shall be inserted—

"(d) in the case of an offence under section 5B(3), 5C(4) or 5D(3), to a fine not exceeding level 3 on the standard scale, and

(e) in the case of an offence under section 5C(5), to a fine not exceeding level 1 on the standard scale.".

Minor amendment

8. Section 3(9) (notice varying order about sale or supply of intoxicating liquor) shall have effect, and be taken always to have had effect, as if in paragraph (*b*) " order " read " notice ".

Part II

Scotland

Introduction

1980 c. 62.   9. Part V of the Criminal Justice (Scotland) Act 1980 (sporting events: control of alcohol etc.) shall be amended as mentioned in this Part.

Vehicles

10. After section 70 there shall be inserted the following—

"Alcohol on certain other vehicles.   70A.—(1) This section applies to a motor vehicle which is not a public service vehicle but is adapted to carry more than 8 passengers and is being operated for the principal purpose of conveying two or more passengers for the whole or part of a journey to or from a designated sporting event.

(2) Any person in possession of alcohol on a vehicle to which this section applies shall be guilty of an offence and liable on summary conviction to imprisonment for a period not exceeding 60 days or a fine not exceeding level 3 on the standard scale or both.

(3) Any person who is drunk on a vehicle to which this section applies shall be guilty of an offence and liable on summary conviction to a fine not exceeding level 2 on the standard scale.

(4) Any person who permits alcohol to be carried on a vehicle to which this section applies and—

(*a*) is the driver of the vehicle, or

(*b*) where he is not its driver, is the keeper of the vehicle, the employee or agent of the keeper, a person to whom it is made available (by hire, loan or otherwise) by the keeper or the keeper's employee or agent, or the employee or agent of a person to whom it is so made available,

shall, subject to section 71 of this Act, be guilty of an offence and liable on summary conviction to a fine not exceeding level 3 on the standard scale.".

11. In section 71 (defences in connection with carriage of alcohol) for " or 70 " there shall be substituted ", 70 or 70A(4) ".

12. In section 75 (police powers of enforcement) for " or 70 " there shall be substituted ", 70 or 70A ".

13. In section 77 (interpretation of Part V)—   Sch. 1

(*a*) the following definitions shall be inserted in the appropriate places alphabetically—

" " keeper ", in relation to a vehicle, means the person having the duty to take out a licence for it under section 1(1) of the Vehicles (Excise) Act 1971 ;   1971 c. 10.

" motor vehicle " means a mechanically propelled vehicle intended or adapted for use on roads ; " ; and

(*b*) in the definition of " public service vehicle " for the words " Part I of the Transport Act 1980 " there shall be substituted the words " the Public Passenger Vehicles Act 1981 c. 14. 1981 " ; ".

Fireworks etc.

14.—(1) After section 72 there shall be inserted the following—

" Possession of fireworks etc. at sporting events.

72A.—(1) Any person who has entered the relevant area of a designated sports ground and is in possession of a controlled article or substance at any time during the period of a designated sporting event shall be guilty of an offence.

(2) Any person who, while in possession of a controlled article or substance, attempts to enter the relevant area of a designated sports ground at any time during the period of a designated sporting event at the ground shall be guilty of an offence.

(3) A person guilty of an offence under subsection (1) or (2) above shall be liable on summary conviction to imprisonment for a period not exceeding 60 days or to a fine not exceeding level 3 on the standard scale or both.

(4) It shall be a defence for a person charged with an offence under subsection (1) or (2) above to show that he had lawful authority to be in possession of the controlled article or substance.

(5) In subsections (1) and (2) above " controlled article or substance " means—

(*a*) any article or substance whose main purpose is the emission of a flare for purposes of illuminating or signalling (as opposed to igniting or heating) or the emission of smoke or a visible gas ; and in particular it includes distress flares, fog signals, and pellets and capsules intended to be used as fumigators or for testing pipes, but not matches, cigarette lighters or heaters ; and

(*b*) any article which is a firework.".

(2) In section 75 (police powers of enforcement) at the end of sub-paragraph (ii) of paragraph (*e*) there shall be inserted—

" ; or

(iii) a controlled article or substance as defined in section 72A(5) of this Act.".

171

SCHEDULE 2

OTHER AMENDMENTS

Conspiracy and Protection of Property Act 1875 (c.86)

1.—(1) In section 7 of the Conspiracy and Protection of Property Act 1875 (offence to intimidate etc. with a view to compelling another to abstain from doing or to do an act) for the words from "shall" to the end there shall be substituted "shall be liable on summary conviction to imprisonment for a term not exceeding 6 months or a fine not exceeding level 5 on the standard scale or both.".

(2) And the following shall be added at the end of that section—

"A constable may arrest without warrant anyone he reasonably suspects is committing an offence under this section.".

Prevention of Crime Act 1953 (c.14)

2. In section 1 of the Prevention of Crime Act 1953 (offence to have offensive weapon) at the end of subsection (4) (offensive weapon includes article intended by person having it for use by him) there shall be added "or by some other person".

Civic Government (Scotland) Act 1982 (c.45)

3.—(1) Part V of the Civic Government (Scotland) Act 1982 (public processions) shall be amended in accordance with this paragraph.

(2) In section 62 (notification of processions)—

(*a*) in subsection (1)—

(i) after "below" there shall be inserted "(*a*)"; and
(ii) at the end there shall be inserted—

"; and

(*b*) to the chief constable.";

(*b*) in subsection (2)—

(i) in paragraph (*a*), after "council" there shall be inserted "and to the office of the chief constable";
(ii) in paragraph (*b*), for "that office" there shall be substituted "those offices";

(*c*) in subsection (4)—

(i) after "area" there shall be inserted "(*a*)"; and
(ii) after "them" there shall be inserted—

"; and

(*b*) intimated to the chief constable."; and

(*d*) in subsection (12), in the definition of "public place", for "the Public Order Act 1936" there shall be substituted "Part II of the Public Order Act 1986".

(3) In section 63 (functions of regional and islands councils in relation to processions)—

(*a*) after subsection (1) there shall be inserted—

" (1A) Where notice of a proposal to hold a procession has been given or falls to be treated as having been given in accordance with section 62(1) of this Act—

(*a*) if a regional or islands council have made an order under subsection (1) above they may at any time thereafter, after consulting the chief constable, vary or revoke the order and, where they revoke it, make any order which they were empowered to make under that subsection ;

(*b*) if they have decided not to make an order they may at any time thereafter, after consulting the chief constable, make any order which they were empowered to make under that subsection." ;

(*b*) in subsection (2) after " (1) " there shall be inserted " or (1A) " ;

(*c*) in subsection (3)—

(i) in paragraph (*a*)(i), after "(1)" there shall be inserted or (1A) above " ;

(ii) in paragraph (*a*)(ii), for " such an order " there shall be substituted " an order under subsection (1) above or to revoke an order already made under subsection (1) or (1A) above " ;

(iii) at the end of paragraph (*a*)(ii), for " and " there shall be substituted—

" (iii) where they have, under subsection (1A) above, varied such an order, a copy of the order as varied and a written statement of the reasons for the variation ; and " ;

(iv) in paragraph (*b*), after " (1) ", there shall be inserted " or (1A) ", and after " made " where third occurring there shall be inserted " and, if the order has been varied under subsection (1A) above, that it has been so varied " ; and

(v) at the end of paragraph (*b*) there shall be inserted—
" ; and

(*c*) where they have revoked an order made under subsection (1) or (1A) above in relation to a proposal to hold a procession, make such arrangements as will ensure that persons who might take or are taking part in that procession are made aware of the fact that the order has been revoked.".

(4) In section 64 (appeals against orders under section 63)—

(a) in subsection (1) for the words from " against " to the end there shall be substituted—

" against—

(a) an order made under section 63(1) or (1A) of this Act ; or

(b) a variation under section 63(1A) of this Act of an order made under section 63(1) or (1A), in relation to the procession." ;

(b) in subsection (4) after " make " there shall be inserted " or, as the case may be, to vary " ; and

(c) in subsection (7) after " order " there shall be inserted " or, as the case may be, the variation of whose order ".

(5) In section 65 (offences and enforcement)—

(a) in paragraphs (b) and (c) of subsection (1), after " (1) " there shall be inserted " or (1A) " ; and

(b) in paragraphs (b) and (c) of subsection (2), after " (1) " there shall be inserted " or (1A) ".

(6) In section 66 (relationship with Public Order Act 1936)—

(a) for " the Public Order Act 1936 " there shall be substituted " Part II of the Public Order Act 1986 " ;

(b) in paragraph (a), for " or order made under section 3 " there shall be substituted " under section 12 ", and " or that order " shall be omitted ; and

(c) in paragraph (b), " or order under the said section 3 " shall be omitted.

Criminal Justice Act 1982 (c.48)

4. The following shall be inserted at the end of Part II of Schedule 1 to the Criminal Justice Act 1982 (statutory offences excluded from provisions for early release of prisoners)—

PUBLIC ORDER ACT 1986

27. Section 1 (riot).
28. Section 2 (violent disorder).
29. Section 3 (affray).".

Cable and Broadcasting Act 1984 (c.46)

5.—(1) The Cable and Broadcasting Act 1984 as it extends to England and Wales and Scotland is amended as follows.

(2) Omit section 27 (inclusion of programme in cable programme service likely to stir up racial hatred).

(3) In section 28 (amendment of the law of defamation), at the end add—

" (6) In this section " words " includes pictures, visual images, gestures and other methods of signifying meaning.".

(4) In section 33(2), in the definition of "relevant offence" omit "an offence under section 27 above or ".   Sᴄʜ. 2

6.—(1) Section 27 of the Cable and Broadcasting Act 1984 as it extends to Northern Ireland is amended as follows.

(2) For subsections (1) to (5) substitute—

" (1) If a programme involving threatening, abusive or insulting visual images or sounds is included in a cable programme service, each of the persons mentioned in subsection (2) below is guilty of an offence if—

(a) he intends thereby to stir up racial hatred, or

(b) having regard to all the circumstances racial hatred is likely to be stirred up thereby.

(2) The persons are—

(a) the person providing the cable programme service,

(b) any person by whom the programme is produced or directed, and

(c) any person by whom offending words or behaviour are used.

(3) If the person providing the service, or a person by whom the programme was produced or directed, is not shown to have intended to stir up racial hatred, it is a defence for him to prove that—

(a) he did not know and had no reason to suspect that the programme would involve the offending material, and

(b) having regard to the circumstances in which the programme was included in a cable programme service, it was not reasonably practicable for him to secure the removal of the material.

(4) It is a defence for a person by whom the programme was produced or directed who is not shown to have intended to stir up racial hatred to prove that he did not know and had no reason to suspect—

(a) that the programme would be included in a cable programme service, or

(b) that the circumstances in which the programme would be so included would be such that racial hatred would be likely to be stirred up.

(5) It is a defence for a person by whom offending words or behaviour were used and who is not shown to have intended to stir up racial hatred to prove that he did not know and had no reason to suspect—

(a) that a programme involving the use of the offending material would be included in a cable programme service, or

(b) that the circumstances in which a programme involving the use of the offending material would be so included, or in which a programme so included would involve the use of the offending material, would be such that racial hatred would be likely to be stirred up.

(5A) A person who is not shown to have intended to stir up racial hatred is not guilty of an offence under this section if he did not know, and had no reason to suspect, that the offending material was threatening, abusive or insulting.

(5B) A person guilty of an offence under this section is liable—

(*a*) on conviction on indictment to imprisonment for a term not exceeding two years or a fine or both ;

(*b*) on summary conviction to imprisonment for a term not exceeding six months or a fine not exceeding the statutory maximum or both.".

(3) In subsection (8) (consents to prosecutions), for the words from " shall not be instituted " to the end substitute " shall not be instituted except by or with the consent of the Attorney General for Northern Ireland.".

(4) In subsection (9) (interpretation) for " ' racial group ' means a group of persons " substitute " ' racial hatred ' means hatred against a group of persons in Northern Ireland ".

(5) After subsection (10) insert—
" (11) This section extends to Northern Ireland only.".

Police and Criminal Evidence Act 1984 (c.60)
7. In section 17(1)(*c*) of the Police and Criminal Evidence Act 1984 (entry for purpose of arrest for certain offences) in sub-paragraph (i) the words from " 4 " to " peace) " shall be omitted and after sub-paragraph (ii) there shall be inserted—
" (iii) section 4 of the Public Order Act 1986 (fear or provocation of violence) ; ".

Section 40(3).

SCHEDULE 3
REPEALS

Chapter	Short title	Extent of repeal
13 Chas. 2. Stat. 1. c. 5.	Tumultuous Petitioning Act 1661.	The whole Act.
33 Geo. 3. c. 67.	Shipping Offences Act 1793.	The whole Act.
57 Geo. 3. c. 19.	Seditious Meetings Act 1817.	The whole Act.
5 Geo. 4. c. 83.	Vagrancy Act 1824.	In section 4, the words from " every person being armed " to " arrestable offence " and from " and every such gun " to the end.
2 & 3 Vict. c. 47.	Metropolitan Police Act 1839.	In section 54, paragraph 13.
2 & 3 Vict. c. xciv.	City of London Police Act 1839.	In section 35, paragraph 13.

Chapter	Short title	Extent of repeal
3 Edw. 7.c .ccl.	Erith Tramways and Improvement Act 1903.	Section 171.
1 Edw. 8 & 1 Geo. 6. c. 6.	Public Order Act 1936.	Section 3. Section 4. Section 5. Section 5A. In section 7, in subsection (2) the words " or section 5 or 5A " and in subsection (3) the words " , four or five ". Section 8 (6). In section 9, in subsection (1) the definition of " public procession " and in subsection (3) the words " by the council of any borough or district or ".
7 & 8 Geo. 6. c.xxi.	Middlesex County Council Act 1944.	Section 309.
1967 c. 58.	Criminal Law Act 1967.	Section 11(3). In Schedule 2, paragraph 2(1) (*b*).
1968 c. 54.	Theatres Act 1968.	Section 5. In sections 7(2), 8, 9(1), 10 (1) (*a*) and (*b*), 15(1)(*a*) and 18(2), the references to section 5.
1976 c. 74.	Race Relations Act 1976.	Section 70. Section 79(6).
1976 c. xxxv.	County of South Glamorgan Act 1976.	Section 25. In Part I of Schedule 3, the entry relating to section 25.
1980 c. 62.	Criminal Justice (Scotland) Act 1980.	In section 75(*e*)(i), the word " or " at the end.
1980 c. x.	County of Merseyside Act 1980.	In section 30(2), paragraph (*b*), the word " and " preceding that paragraph and the words from " and may make " to the end. In section 30(5), the words " in the said section 31 or " Section 31. In section 137(2), the reference to section 31.
1980 c. xi.	West Midlands County Council Act 1980.	Section 38, except subsection (4). In section 116(2), the reference to section 38.
1980 c. xiii.	Cheshire County Council Act 1980.	Section 28, except subsection (4). In section 108(2), the reference to section 28.
1980 c. xv.	Isle of Wight Act 1980.	Section 26, except subsection (4). In section 63(2), the reference to section 26.
1981 c. ix.	Greater Manchester Act 1981.	Section 56, except subsection (4). In section 179(2), the reference to section 56.

Chapter	Short title	Extent of repeal
1981 c. xxv.	East Sussex Act 1981.	Section 29. In section 102(2), the reference to section 29.
1982 c. 45.	Civic Government (Scotland) Act 1982.	Section 62(10). In section 63(3)(*a*)(i), the word " or " at the end. In section 66, in paragraph (*a*), the words " or that order ", and in paragraph (*b*) the words " or order under the said section 3 ".
1982 c. 48.	Criminal Justice Act 1982.	In Part I of Schedule 1, the entries relating to riot and affray.
1984 c. 46.	Cable and Broadcasting Act 1984.	Section 27. In section 33 (2), the words "an offence under section 27 above or".
1984 c. 60.	Police and Criminal Evidence Act 1984.	In section 17(1)(*c*)(i) the words from " 4 " to " peace) ".
1985 c. 57.	Sporting Events (Control of Alcohol etc.) Act 1985.	In section 8, the word " and " at the end of paragraph (*b*).

PRINTED IN ENGLAND BY W. J. SHARP, CB
Controller and Chief Executive of Her Majesty's Stationery Office and
Queen's Printer of Acts of Parliament

Appendix B

Specimen prohibition order

Reproduced by arrangement with Leicester City Council

LEICESTER CITY COUNCIL
PUBLIC ORDER ACT 1936

WHEREAS Alan Goodson, the Chief Officer of Police for the County of Leicestershire, being of the opinion that by reason of particular circumstances existing in the City of Leicester, the powers conferred on him by sub-section (1) of Section 3 of the Public Order Act, 1936, will not be sufficient to enable him to prevent serious public disorder being occasioned by the holding of public processions in that City, has applied to the Leicester City Council for an Order prohibiting from 6.00 a.m. on Saturday 2nd February 1985 to 6.00 a.m. on Monday 11th February 1985 the holding of all public processions in the said City except those of a religious, educational, festive or ceremonial character customarily held in the said City:

AND WHEREAS the Secretary of State has signified to the said Council his consent to the said Order:

NOW THEREFORE in pursuance of sub-section (2) of Section 3 of the Public Order Act, 1936, the Leicester City Council, with the consent of the Secretary of State, HEREBY ORDER that the holding of all public processions in the City of Leicester except those of a religious, educational, festive or ceremonial character customarily held in the said City, shall be prohibited from 6.00 a.m. on Saturday 2nd February 1985 to 6.00 a.m. on Monday 11th Febuary 1985.

(Sealed etc)

Appendix C

Control of street processions: Code of Practice issued by West Midlands Police

Reproduced by arrangement with the West Midlands police

CONTROL OF STREET PROCESSIONS

CODE OF PRACTICE

1   This Code of Practice is issued in accordance with Section 38 of the West Midlands County Council Act, 1980, in order to give guidance to organisers of processions, with a view to furthering co-operation between them and the police and to ensuring that such events pass off successfully but at the same time with the minimum of inconvenience to the public at large.

2   Legal Requirements

(a)   It is an offence for any person to organise or conduct a procession through any street unless there has been served on the Chief Officer of Police at any police station in the district through which the procession is intended to pass, a notice stating the route by which and the date and time on and at which it is intended that it should pass.

(b)   Notice under paragraph (a) above shall be served at a time not less than 72 hours before the procession starts to pass through any street or as soon as reasonably practicable after that time.

If any procession passes through any street in a district by a route or at a time which has not been stated in the notice (except in accordance with directions given by the Chief Officer of Police under Section 3 of the Public Order Act 1936 or other directions given by the senior police officer attending the procession) any person organising or conducting the procession shall be guilty of an offence.

3   Exemptions from Legal Requirements

The requirement to give notice does not apply to a procession:

(a)   commonly or customarily held or

(b)   organised or conducted for the purpose of a funeral by a person acting in the normal course of his business where his business is that of a funeral director.

Organisers of processions which are exempt from the legal requirement to give notice are asked to notify the police if the normal traffic flow is likely to be disrupted.

4   Early Notice of Procession

It will be of mutual benefit to the police and the organisers in planning a procession if notice of the event is given to the police at the earliest possible opportunity. Experience has shown that organisers of processions have found the advice and guidance given by the police to be of value in planning the event.

180

5   Police Powers in Preserving Law and Order

Organisers and persons taking part in demonstrations and processions should be aware of the powers made available to the police to preserve law and order and the Queen's Peace. These include the following provisions:-

(a)   It is an offence for any person to possess an offensive weapon at any public meeting or on the occasion of any public procession other than in pursuance of lawful authority.

(b)   It is an offence in any public place or at any public meeting to use threatening, abusive or insulting words or behaviour or to distribute or display any writing, sign or visible representation which is threatening, abusive or insulting with intent to provoke a breach of the peace or whereby a breach of the peace is likely to be occasioned.

(c)   It is an offence to incite racial hatred by:

    (i)   publishing or distributing written matter which is threatening abusive or insulting
    or

    (ii)   using in any public place or at any public meeting words which are threatening, abusive or insulting

where, having regard to all the circumstances, hatred is likely to be stirred up against any racial group in Great Britain by the matter or words in question.

6   Information Requested from Organisers

Persons wishing to organise a procession are advised to notify the police either in writing, if time permits, or by calling at a police station in the area where the procession is to take place. In most cases organisers will be asked to meet with senior police officers to discuss the proposed procession/ demonstration when any matters upon which the organisers are not clear or would wish to seek further advice can be resolved.

Organisers will be requested to provide information covering the following points:-

(a)   the name of the organisation

(b)   the name and address of the organiser or organising committee together with telephone numbers to provide ready means of contact to discuss any developments

(c)   place of assembly

(d)   time and date of assembly

(e)   parking facilities for those taking part in the procession — coaches and private vehicles

(f)   the names of person(s) who will be in charge at the assembly area

(g)   the time the procession is to move off

(h)   the proposed route and destination

(i)   the number and size of vehicles/floats in a mobile procession

(j)   vehicles accompanying the march — in the interests of safety vehicles will only be permitted at the front and rear of marches, never in the main body (the provision of a suitable vehicle at the rear of the procession may be of assistance to the organisers to cater for the conveyance of invalids who wish to give support, to provide transport for persons suffering fatigue or disability during the procession, the provision of simple first aid facilities for blisters etc.)

(k)   the number of persons expected to take part in the procession

(l)   whether a meeting is to be held before/after the procession

(m)   the venue of any meeting

(n)   time of dispersal

(o)   parking facilities for coaches/private cars in the vicinity of the dispersal point

(p)   whether permission has been granted for private property to be used in connection with the procession or demonstration, e.g. permission from Local Authority to use park for assembly area

(q)   whether any organisation is likely to demonstrate in opposition

(r)   the number of stewards to be provided

(s)   whether flags, banners or emblems are to be carried

(t)   the name of the person who may be consulted by the police should the occasion arise during the course of the procession, and where that person can be found during the movement

7   Guidance to Organisers on Employment of Stewards

Stewards should be appointed to assist the organiser at the rate of one to every 50 persons taking part. It must be emphasised that a steward acts as a private person and cannot acquire or be delegated police powers or authority nor any immunity from the law.

In order to retain control of the procession it is suggested that organisers should establish a chain of command for stewards who should know to whom they are responsible and to whom they can refer matters for decision.

Stewards should be readily identifiable as such by all persons taking part in the event. Previous experience has shown that the wearing of lapel badges alone is not sufficient identification and it is suggested that distinctive clothing or arm-bands should be worn.

Stewards should clearly understand that they are acting as private persons and their status does not confer any advantage in law nor allow them to act as police officers in any way. They should not become involved themselves in any incident which is likely to lead to breaches of the law or public disorder. They must refer such incidents to the police immediately.

Stewards should be reminded that the carrying of a weapon in any public place without lawful authority or reasonable excuse is prohibited by law. This includes the possession of such a weapon as a deterrent. Stewards must not carry or have with or near them any such weapons.

8   Duties of Stewards

Stewards should confine themselves to acting on the instructions given by members of the organising committee or on directions or advice received from police.

The police have a duty to avoid breaches of the peace where possible and on occasions have to direct a procession by another route. Accordingly, should the instructions given to the steward by those organising the event conflict with instructions given to the steward by the police officers on the scene, the steward should be reminded that should he persist in following the original instructions he might be in jeopardy of committing an offence of obstructing the police in the execution of their duty.

Stewards should carry out their duties with tact and good humour especially when handling or defusing potentially difficult situations. Persons taking part in a procession are more likely to respond favourably to organisers and their stewards who display the ability to control the event and guide the participants. The response is most likely to be achieved if stewards ensure that they give participants clear and accurate directions and advice. It is important therefore that the stewards themselves are properly and fully briefed about their duties.

9   Confirmation of Agreed Route and Arrangements

The police will inform the organiser(s) in writing confirming the arrangements and the route to be followed subject to the proviso that the route may be varied by police either before or during the event if considered necessary in the light of any unforeseen developments.

January 1986

G J DEAR
Chief Constable

Index